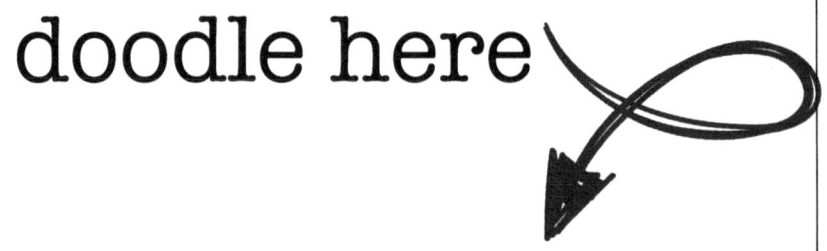

Iris Jonas is a typical ten year old girl trying to figure out where her artistic confidence is. She loves to create in a variety of ways. One day in math class, she is sent to the office for doodling on her homework. Little did she know, her teacher was really sending her to a magical place called OMNIFICLAND. This journey will change her in many ways. She travels through several creative places that she never knew existed. These places help Iris find herself, and she also finds a friend in a boy named Henley. They meet in OMNIFICLAND and have to find their way back to school together.

OMNIFICLAND

This book is dedicated to all of my creative family, friends and students. I have always loved to create. I have learned how to be creative from my family. So this is for the doodlers, scribblers, and creators of all kinds of art.

This book is *also* meant to doodle, draw, scribble, color and create. *There are large spaces in the margins just for creating.*

omnificent – creating all things; having unlimited powers of creation

doodle here

Table of Contents

Chapter 1 – The Reason
Chapter 2 – The White Chair
Chapter 3 – The Dice of OMNIFICLAND
Chapter 4 – Another One Bites the Dust
Chapter 5 – The Artist's Playlist
Chapter 6 – The Weeping Willows
Chapter 7 – Writing Whereabouts Words
Chapter 8 – The Painted Dogs
Chapter 9 – The Blue Dasher Dragon Flies
Chapter 10 – Paintbrush Forest
Chapter 11 – The Wool Transit
Chapter 12 – The Quilter's Message
Chapter 13 – The Gift Shop
Chapter 14 – The Journal's Post Its
Chapter 15 – Mrs. Pepper's Lesson
Chapter 16 – The True Hallway of Artists
Chapter 17 – The Kindness of a Rock
Chapter 18 – Lesson from the Loafers
Chapter 19 – The Mural of Mistakes
Chapter 20 – Perfecting Your Craft

1 The Reason

It happened so many times before. Teachers would tell me, "Iris, stop doodling on your homework." I couldn't help it. Art was alive in me. No matter how hard I tried not to doodle, I would do it anyways. It was an instinct and it was in my blood. No really, it is in my blood! Soooooo many of my family members have the gift of some kind of art in them. I have learned from some of the BEST! It is the REASON I doodle and create.

Let me give you a little background on my amazing and artsy family. This may take some time. I told you, A LOT of my family has talent in some creative way.

My aunts Maureen and Beth are water color painters. I have always thought, it is so amazing how they can mix water with any color and create such realistic portraits. They make them so life like, almost like a photograph. You have to mix the exact amount of color, water and more color. Water color brushes, paper and layering the colors is very important when it comes to water color. My aunts have mastered the techniques and they know all the tricks.

My aunt Sara has the talent of speaking in public. I always wonder if she ever gets nervous. She has created a book and a company to help people work better together. She wants others to see each other and treat each other equally. She speaks in such a manner to make you laugh WITH her and understand her point. She stands her ground on what is important to her. I love her confidence and passion for speaking.

My uncles Tim and Dan create with lumber. They can build anything! They can build houses, decks, or bird houses. The way they can see and design is beyond me. A lot of math goes into building. You need to know angles, measurements, and how it all fits together. They are good at using big tools and are not afraid to get their hands dirty. I think they learned their woodworking skills a bit from my grandpa.

My uncle Kevin has the gift of song. He can sing like a bird. I am always impressed with how long he can hold a note. He also is great at planning and organizing thoughts. He sees people's talents and guides them to success. He has a true gift of listening and inquiring about people's strengths and talents.

My aunt Ann has a gift of design and planning parties. She can make any event into a room full of smiling people. She is really good at organizing ideas the making them come to life. She certainly has an eye for design and color. She can stylishly decorate any space with grace and ease.

My aunt Leisha is so fun! She can create things out of nothing. I mean like take a glass jar and a tin can and she makes it into art or useful in some way. I have heard the expression that one man's trash is another man's treasure. My aunt Leisha gets that! It is fun to create things from garbage or empty jars. I mean, why not? Have you ever created anything from duct tape? Now that is fun! She really sees the value of simple things. She treasures everything and everyone who means a lot to her.

    My aunt Kate is very crafty too. She makes all kinds of fun things. She sews, crafts and her love is with gardening in her yard. She exudes so much joy for people. This is an art in itself. She is always going out of her way to make people feel special. Her imagination to entertain is creative and expressive.

    She loves flowers and planting veggies. This is also a passion of my mom, Beth, Maureen and many others in my family. The natural beauty of flowers is all art. Have you ever really looked at flowers? There are so many different colors in flowers. So many shapes and textures in flowers. I love how different flowers can look together in a vase or bouquet. The flowers make a creation that smells good and brightens the room. I think they all got that love of flowers from my grandmother.

    My mom, Mary Carol is a creator with fabric. She puts together the most colorful and vibrant quilts you could find. I wondered how she could take cut-up bits of fabric to make geometric masterpieces. People are always in awe of her quilted creations. My grandmother also had the gift of quilting, but she exuded so much positive energy towards gardening, sewing, cooking, baking and many other joys. I always loved how she would hum or sing while doing such talents.

My aunts, uncles and mom definitely inherited these traits from her. My dad is a creator of words. He can create poems that make you laugh or cry. Sometimes both at the same time. You should see us all at Christmas. Everyone makes gifts for everyone.

SO YOU SEE... I HAVE NO CHANCE!

With all these creative minds that have come before me... How could I possibly NOT doodle? I just think about how there is such a variety of ways to express yourself creatively. I love drawing, of course. I also like painting, sewing, photography, making bracelets, making jewelry, and so much more.

I even recently started collecting stamps. When you think about it, stamps are little artistic creations. Every stamp is a work of art expressing something important. A stamp is a little piece of paper honoring a person, place or thing. It was something that was easy to start collecting, since my dad is a postal worker. I love when he comes home with a new stamp for me. I just love organized them in binders.

My sisters and I love music and dancing. We are often found creating choreography to our favorite songs. Our favorite place to create dance is in the drive way. The neighbors are entertained daily with our composed motions. Our mom put us in 4-H so that we could truly create and be proud of our creations by showing them in the county fair. We enter projects in sewing, painting, drawing, baking and so much more.

I am a bit self-conscious yet with my creations. I have such idols in my family that I try to live up to. I think often, am I good enough? That is why I needed to practice whenever I could. I need to get better at my craft. I am still trying to figure out what that is exactly.

Don't get me wrong. I like school. I like learning. I just tend to get distracted with my creative mind and hand. On this particular day in fourth grade, we were doing a math lesson on symmetry. Just the thought of symmetry got me wanting to draw.

I just love drawing and color! My name Iris, means Goddess of the Rainbow. I guess rainbows are universal signs for hope and promise. They assure us that there is beauty and clarity following times of doubt. See I told you, I really have no chance. How am I not supposed to doodle with a name that means Goddess of the Rainbow?

Anyways, my teacher was showing us how to make symmetrical shapes. You can make shapes symmetrical vertically, horizontally and also like a kaleidoscope, all the way around. I think Mrs. Pepper said that means the shape has radial symmetry. In the middle of the lesson, I started doodling again on the edge of my paper. Mrs. Pepper came up to me and said, "Iris, will you please go to the principal's office?"

Oh great! Here we go! Now I was in trouble. I complied by standing up. Mrs. Pepper gave me a notecard with the word **OMNIFICLAND** on it. The word was in BOLD bubble letters. There were many colors on it. Each letter seemed to be a different color or shade of the rainbow. She told me to take the card to the office and hand it to the secretary.

I didn't say anything and walked slowly to the office. I looked at the card. **OMNIFICLAND**
What in the world did I get myself into?
What was I going to tell my parents?
Would they understand? What would the secretary do when I handed her this card that said... OMNIFICLAND? I wondered, what does this word mean? Land is at the end of the word.
Does that mean I was being sent to a place? Oh my gosh, I thought. I bet it was an awful place that doodlers were sent to. How was I going to get out of this?

As I was walking to the office one of my best friends Josie snuck up behind me. She asked me where I was going. I didn't want her to know I was in trouble. I hid the OMNIFICLAND card behind my back and I told her I was running an errand for the teacher. She waved good bye as if the whole world was peachy.

The halls seemed to go on forever. Everyone looked so normal, going about their day as nothing was wrong. Couldn't they see that I was being sent to the office for *no reason*? I turned down one more hallway. This hallway lead to the office. It was a long stretch of a hallway. It is one hallway that I always LOVE to go down. It is full of amazing framed artwork. On each piece of art is a name. I think they have been collecting them for years. No matter how many times I look at them, I find them fascinating. I think there has to be at least 75 framed pieces of art. Each piece is different and unique in their own way. The art helped me forget about where I was going and why for just a moment.

I just couldn't believe that I got sent to the office for doodling. I mean, my teacher isn't that bad. I actually kind of like Mrs. Pepper. She even has us do art in her room occasionally. Sometimes she lets us draw or work on the iPad with art. We have a mural wall made of a large piece of paper. When we are working quietly as a class, she will let a few of us create something on the mural. She just taps you on the shoulder and we know that means we can go draw on the wall if we want to. Most of the time she doesn't mind my doodles. I guess that wasn't the case this time.

As I approached the office, I could see the secretary working diligently at her desk. She was on the phone as I got closer. Her name is Mrs. Walker. She is the BEST secretary in town. She always gives you hugs and never looks upset. I wondered if she would be disappointed when I handed her this card. Would she know what this word means? Would she ask me what it meant? I wasn't sure how she would act. I waited silently and stood very still as I waited for her to get off the phone.

No one else was around as I was waiting. Usually the office is hopping with teachers, students, and our principal Mrs. Grizzly. I wondered if I would have to talk to Mrs. Grizzly. Would she call my parents? My mind was full of questions as I waited for Mrs. Walker.

As I was in my thoughts I heard someone say, "Hello Iris." It was Mrs. Walker.

She was smiling and offering me a hug by opening her arms out wide. I gave her a hug and a half smile. She always had a wonderful flowery smell to her, and her hugs were so warm. She asked, "What can I do for you, my dear?" I handed her the card.

    I closed my eyes tight in hopes that it would disappear. I felt her take the card from my hand. I slowly opened my eyes. First my right eye, then my left. I saw her walking to the principal's office. I followed her. She told me to have a seat on the white chair in the hall.

    Then she went back to her desk to work. What was I supposed to do? I wondered if I would be in the office all day. There was another student sitting on the yellow chair next to the office. This student was often in *THAT* yellow chair. Our class would walk by and he always seemed to be in *THAT* yellow chair. Now that I think of it... I never really saw anyone sitting in the white chair.

    One time, about a week ago I saw Henley Roberts sitting in the white chair. He is a student in my class. He is very musical and is often tapping his pencil to the beat of songs he likes. We have that in common. I LOVE music. Now that I think of it, I hadn't seen Henley in a while. Where had he been? Why was he sitting on the white chair a couple days ago, and what happened to him?

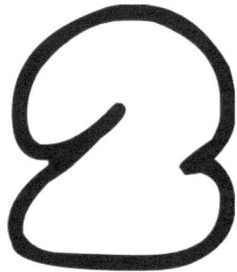

The White Chair

    As I sat in the white chair I noticed it had unique patterns etched and carved in it. I followed the patterns with my finger to calm myself down. I was amazed at how someone could carve such a unique pattern in a chair like that. I wondered if there were more chairs like this one or was it a one of a kind. It looked like something one of my uncles could build. I don't think I was sitting there for too long, when Mrs. Grizzly tapped me on the shoulder.

    She motioned for me to follow her. We went to her office. She was holding the ONMIFICLAND card in her hand. She didn't seem happy or upset. She was just very quiet and calm. I really like Mrs. Grizzly. She has a lot of positive energy and is always kind. She has a loud laugh that we often hear throughout the day because she is just a happy person.

    She handed me a journal with the word ONMINFICLAND on it. She looked at me with intention, as if I was to understand what was about to happen.

The journal was very unique. It was made of leather, and had paisley impressions on it. It had a brown band to keep it closed. A detachable drawing pencil was on a string and attached to the journal. The whole thing was quite beautiful. As I was inspecting the journal, Mrs. Grizzly moved to a corner in her office. I have not been in Mrs. Grizzly's office many times. I have never noticed that she has a small door in the corner of her office.

You almost don't see it because the door is the same color as the wall. It is also a short door. The top of the door was at my shoulders. She motioned for me to go to the door. She said, "You are about to go on a journey like no other. OMNIFICLAND is a place where you will learn a lesson. You will learn your path."

I looked at her in a confused way. Where was I about to go? I was really going to go to OMNIFICLAND? She told me to go through the door. I looked at her. I was very unsure. Holding my OMNICLAND journal, I put my hand on the doorknob. It was an old fashioned door knob. It was round and had a checkered pattern on it. I had a good feeling in my stomach as I held the door knob. Something amazing was about to happen. I opened the door, ducked, and walked into a small room. The door shut behind me. I realized I was the only one in this small room.

There was an elevator door in front of me. The elevator was a magnificent rose gold color. There was an outline of a map painted in black on the rose gold color. Three buttons were on the left side of the elevator doors. The buttons looked different than normal elevator buttons. The top button was a circle shape. The top half of the circle was black, with the word Black on it. The bottom part of the button was white, with the word white on it. The second button was a square and it was all grey. The third button was a rectangle with a colorful patterned design on it. On the right side of the elevator it said OMNIFICLAND in a vertical way from the top of the ceiling to the floor. The word was painted in black with a rose gold outline. A Mona Lisa replica painting was hanging to the left of the elevator.

    I can honestly say that this was the strangest thing that I had ever seen. It was like I was dreaming the whole situation. A small sign by the buttons said... Choose the button that you wish to explore. What was I going to explore? Where would it take me? I didn't think that Mrs. Grizzly or Mrs. Walker would put me in a dangerous situation. Mrs. Pepper was always kind. She must have a reason for starting all this.

    There must be a lesson in all of this. I needed to pick a button, but which one? I decided to go with my gut and pick the black and white button. I nervously brought my finger to push the circle button. When I pushed it, it made a guitar sound. Did that mean I picked the right one?

    The doors slowly opened. I stepped into the elevator. There was a white bench with a seatbelt. A voice coming from the elevator speaker said to sit and buckle in. I did what it said. The doors slowly shut. As soon as the doors shut, music started to play. It was the song *Black and White* by Michael Jackson. I think the elevator went down. It had to have went down. Our school is only one floor. I tapped my foot instinctively to the

Michael Jackson song. The elevator was moving for about a minute. When the elevator came to a stop, the music stopped as well. The elevator voice said, "Please unfasten your seatbelt, and exit the elevator. Welcome to Black and White Circle. Enjoy your visit."

As I looked out of the elevator door and stood up, I realized everything was black or white. EVERYTHING! I saw no color. It reminded me of how Dorothy stepped into the Munchkin Land and it was full of color. This was the opposite though. I was stepping into no color from a colored world. How could this be? Just then I heard someone say something, but I didn't see a person anywhere. Again, I heard "Welcome to Black and White Circle."

The only thing I saw moving in front of me was an over-sized, black Sharpie. Sure enough, I looked a little closer and the Sharpie was talking.

She said, "Hello, I am Sharpay, the Sharpie."

Sharpay was very friendly. She asked me if it was my first time visiting Black and White Circle. I assured her that I had never been in this place before. I was convinced this all must be some kind of dream.

Everything in Black and White Circle was Black and White. There was no trace of colors or even greys. ONLY Black or White!! EVEN ME! I was all black and white. I didn't understand how this was happening, but it was.

I asked Sharpay if we were in OMNIFICLAND. She assured me that we were in OMNIFICLAND. We were only in a small portion of it though. In Black and White Circle you have to put on a new set of white loafers. I was a little confused as to why I had to change my shoes, but I figured it should be okay. I took my shoes off and put on the white loafers. Sharpay also gave me a black and white striped bag to put my own shoes in. I also put my OMNIFICLAND leather journal in my bag. After I got my old shoes in the bag and put it on my back, she handed me a black Sharpie.

"Okay!" shouted Sharpay. She was talking like a game show host. "Are you ready for your first OMNIFICLAND test?" she asked.

"TEST? I didn't study for a test. What do I have to do?" I said worriedly. I have never been really good at tests. I have to really study.

"I am going to ask you a series of questions to see where we head to next. Let's go take a seat in the Sharpie Saloon." Sharpay said this as she led me into the Saloon. "Come on in and take a seat at the counter."

The Sharpie Saloon was amazing! All the booths, seats, stools and counters were white. There were thousands of black Sharpies covering the walls. Sharpay told me to take a seat and put my white loafers on the counter where I sat. She told me to open my sharpie and be ready to begin. A test full of questions was placed in front of me, but I was told not to write on it. My answers would be written on my new, white loafers.

I was expected to read the questions and do what the test told me to do based on my answers. I typically did not like tests. They made me nervous. When I got nervous I would just doodle on my tests.

I couldn't write on this test. I wanted to do my best, so that I could move on to the next task. This was definitely a time where I had no clue what was going to happen next. The top of the test said Black & White

Sharpie Test. I placed my white loafers in front of me on the counter.

The directions read...
 For every question that you answer No, put a tally on your left loafer. For every question that you answer YES, draw a flower on your right loafer. There is NO grey area at the Black and White Circle. You must answer YES or NO.

> **Black & White Sharpie Test**
> For every question that you answer NO, put a tally on your left loafer.
> For every question that you answer YES, draw a flower on your right loafer.
> You must answer as YES or NO. There is no grey area at the Black and White Circle.
> 1. Do you like art?
> 2. Do you like to create?
> 3. Do you feel accepted?
> 4. Do you have time for creating art?
> 5. Do you think you are good at art?
> 6. Does art get you in trouble?
> 7. Do you love yourself?
> 8. Do you create something your own every day?
> 9. Do you wish you had more time to create?
> 10. Are you ready to return to your classroom?

 There were several questions under the directions. I quickly scanned the list of questions. This didn't seem so bad. I was confident that I could complete this task.

 The first question was simple! It was an easy YES! It asked if I liked art. I drew a daisy on my right loafer, since my answer was yes. It was weird to draw on the shoes. I had never drawn on shoes before. I felt like I could get in trouble. I continued to the next one. The second question asked if I liked to create. I answered with another flower on my right loafer. This time I drew a tulip.

 The next question was tricky. Do I feel accepted? I had to answer yes or no. NO grey area. I guess if I HAD to answer now, I would say no. I put a tally on my left loafer. Do you have time for creating art was the next question? I guess if I had to say an answer, it would be no. I never have enough time to create. I now had 2 tallies on my left shoe. Number 5 asked if I thought I was good at art. This was a tough one. Sometimes I think I am, but other times I would say no. I decided to answer YES! I drew a rose on my right shoe. So, I now had 3 flowers on my right shoe and 2 tallies on my left shoe.

The sixth question asked if art got me in trouble. Well it was the whole reason I was in this Black and White Circle world. I answered yes with another daisy on my right loafer. Number 7 asked if I love myself. This was another difficult question. I think I am hard on myself, but I think I would answer yes over no. I added a carnation to my collection of flowers. For question 8 I answered no. I do not feel like I create something of my own every day. I was up to 3 tallies. Of course, I answered question 9 with a yes. I always wish I had more time to create. I drew a zinnia on my garden of flowers. I told you my family likes gardening. I know the names and looks of many flowers.

My right loafer was beginning to look like a garden of my grandmothers, minus the color. The last question asked me if I was ready to return to my classroom. Honestly, I wanted to see what was going to happen next in this zebra of a place. I answered question 10 with one more tally. A total of 4 tallies were on my left loafer. Six flowers on my right loafer for a total of my YES answers. I wondered what or where these answers would get me.

I got out my OMNIFICLAND journal to see if it said anything about the black and white test. Magically the flowers I had drawn and the 4 tallies appeared on the first page of my journal. It really was the EXACT flowers I had drawn. This was just so amazing and magical.

On the next page in my journal it said DICE OF OMNIFICLAND on the top of the page. That must be my next task. I put my journal back in my black and white bag. I was ready for what was next.

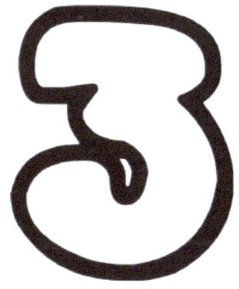

The Dice of OMNIFICLAND

"With 4 tallies and 6 flowers on your loafers, you are ready for the Dice of OMNIFICLAND." Sharpay said excitedly

I wasn't quite sure what to say. Did this mean that I did well on the test? What was the Dice of OMNIFICLAND?

I felt like I was in some giant board game. Sharpay handed me three dice. I looked at her for some assistance. It was like she expected me to know what to do next. I looked at the three unique dice that lay in my hand. I had never seen dice like these. One of the dice had a color on each side. The colors were...

(RED, ORANGE, YELLOW, GREEN, BLUE, PURPLE)

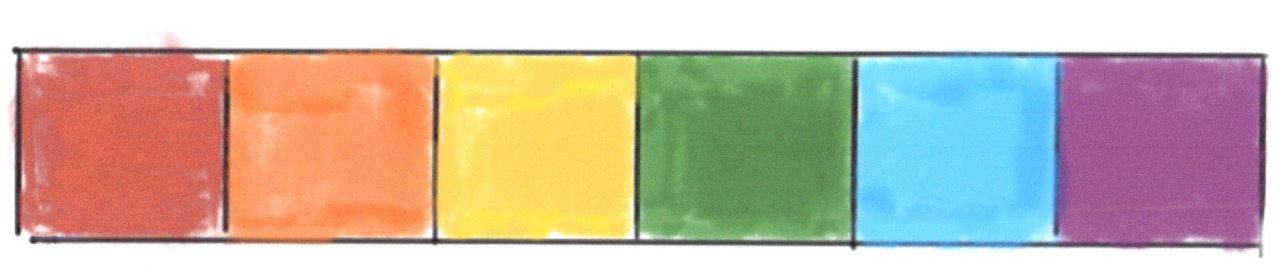

The colors almost glistened and glimmered as if they could light up. The second die had different pictures on each side. At this point the color dice was the only things showing color. The second dice had some black and white pictures on it.

(PAINT PALLOT, PENCIL/ERASER, A SEWING MACHINE, A NOTEBOOK, A TIN CAN, and A BOOM BOX)

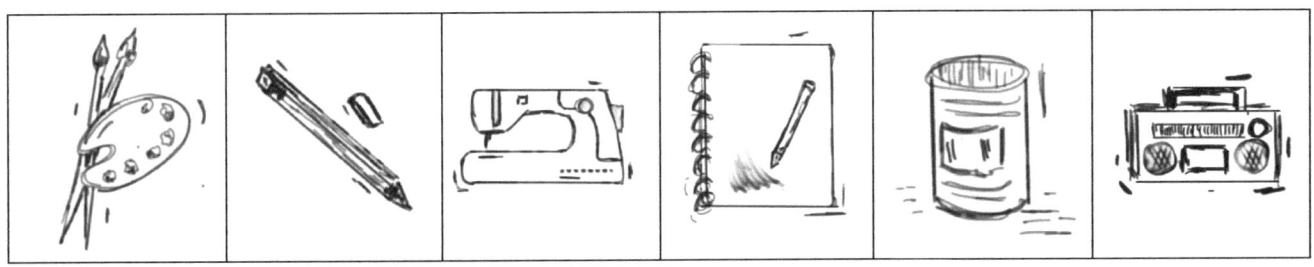

The 3rd die had more black and white pictures on it.
(A CAMERA, A CLAY POT, KNITTING NEEDLES, A DOG, HOUSES, and FLOWERS)

What did these dice mean? I couldn't imagine what would happen next. Many of the pictures got me excited about what could possibly happen next. They were all things I really enjoyed or maybe wanted to learn how to do eventually. I rolled the dice, like Sharpay told me to. The dice landed on PURPLE, BOOMBOX and NOTEBOOK & PENCIL.

Sharpay smiled and said, "It looks like you are headed on Melody Lane which will lead you to Boom Box Cave. This means that you must head down the purple path. This path will be lined with lilac bushes and smells glorious. Oh, and make sure you have your OMNIFICLAND journal, wear your white loafers and take this polaroid camera with you."

I told Sharpay good bye and I thanked her for being so nice and welcoming. We took a quick polaroid selfie and I turned to leave. She then warned me about a villain in OMNIFICLAND.

"He goes by the name of THE ERASER." Sharpay warned. "He only shows up when you show doubt in yourself."

I was excited to get going, but the news of The Eraser made me feel a little scared and uneasy. I did sometimes show doubt in my everyday life. I am sure I would show doubt in this new place. I waved good bye to Sharpay, thanked her and started on my way.

She asked me to go through a tall hedge just beyond the Black and White Circle. The hedge was tall and black. This was odd to me because all hedges I have seen are green. I poked my hand through the black leaves to make sure that I could in fact step through it. My hand went through and I felt the air with my fingers. I slowly eased my way through the black hedge. I squinted, not sure what I would see as I went through. I opened my eyes and everything was back to color. I saw so much purple. There was a long purple brick path. Each side of the path was full of lilac bushes. I smiled at this. I LOVE lilacs. They smell so good. Melody Lane was definitely going to be a fun place. The sky was blue and sun was shining.

This was so weird to me. I was just in school sitting at my desk in Mrs. Pepper's class. Now I was in a magical place after descending in an elevator, and somehow, I was outside.

I took a picture with my polaroid camera to put in my OMNIFICLAND journal. I had to capture this lavender scene. After I snapped the picture, a polaroid did not come out. I thought, it must be broken. I put the camera in my bag and got out my journal. I opened the journal and again, magic! I was impressed to see that the exact picture I just took with the camera was in my journal. It was like instant scrapbooking. Now this could get fun. I put my journal away... excited for what could be next.

ANOTHER ONE BITES THE DUST

    I followed the purple road framed with lilac bushes. I couldn't believe how wonderful the smell was. It made me think of my grandmother, Lucille. She LOVED lilacs and would always pick them and have them in a vase on her table. My mom does that same thing too. She probably learned it from my grandmother. As I followed Lilac Lane I hummed a tune to myself. Then I realized I was humming because I heard music. I looked ahead and saw a tunnel. The music was coming from a huge cave.

    I entered cautiously. As I walked into the tunnel-like cave, I noticed fun lights. Then I noticed that just ahead, the floor was lit up and flashing to music. I also saw a big screen on the tunnel wall. It showed the words… WHAT'S YOUR PLAYLIST in flashing lights, like Broadway. This must be Boom Box Cave!

    I love music and I am very passionate about dancing. Creating dance routines is art too! I love choreographing routines to my favorite songs. This musical place seemed to be right up my alley. Okay… so how did this work? I was excited to see what would happen with this "play list" thing.

    I walked up to the screen. The screen asked me to stand still. Some rays of light scanned my whole body as I stood very still. I wondered why it was doing this. Then the voice chanted the word "calculating" three times in a row. Suddenly everything turned blue with lights. Then the lights started flashing to a beat... HEY! I know this song.

Da Da dah dah dah DUH DUH DUH DUH da da da
da DA da DUH DUH DUH DUH da da da ...

ONE OF MY ALL TIME FAVORITE SONGS!!! Another One Bites the Dust, by Queen! My sisters and I have choreography to this song. Such a classic. The music was so clear and loud that I felt like I was in a Queen concert. The lights made it seem so amazing too. I couldn't help it... I started to dance. The routine my sisters and I made up just started to live in me. As I was dancing, the floor started to move with lights. It was like I was in some crazy dance club. I was having the time of my life in this dancing light cave.

Steve walks warily down the street
With his brim pulled way down low
Ain't no sound but the sound of his feet
Machine guns ready to go
Are you ready hey are you ready for this?
Are you hanging on the edge of your seat?
Out of the doorway the bullets rip
To the sound of the beat yeah

All of a sudden I heard a familiar voice.

"Iris Jonas? Is that you?" someone yelled.

I turned around in mid dance. What? Could this really be happening? The music continued to play loudly as we shouted at each other.

"Henley Roberts? Is that you?" I said surprisingly.

"Iris, what are you doing here?" asked Henley.

Henley looked happy to see me. I wondered how long he had been in OMNIFICLAND. Could it be that he had been here since I saw him sitting on that white chair?

Henley was one of those kids that was nice to everyone. He loved music, just like me. I always thought that I could see us being good friends, but I was a little shy about approaching him. He just had a confidence about him that I never had. That is one thing I always wished I could gain... a little confidence. Of all the people I could meet here in this creative place, I am glad it was Henley Roberts.

Just then the song changed abruptly. The lights changed to a neon green and the song Africa by Toto started to play.

I asked Henley, "What is up with the songs changing? I was just getting into it!"

"It is playing your artist mix tape." He said. "You see, look on the wall."

I looked up on the wall and saw my list. It was in bright neon colors and it was organized by numbering one through ten. I loved seeing my name in the bright neon colors.

Iris Jonas – Artist Playlist
1. Another One Bites the Dust – Queen
2. Africa – Toto
3. Don't Stop Believin' – Journey
4. Sweet Caroline – Neil Diamond
5. Everybody Dance Now – C&C Music Factory
6. The Best – Tina Turner
7. Let's Dance – David Bowie
8. I Wanna Dance With Somebody- Whitney Houston
9. Best of My Love – The Emotions
10.   O-o-h Child – The Five Stair Steps

There it was. Another one of favorite songs glowing in bright green on the wall. I loved this one by Toto! The mixed tape outline had my name on it. Iris Jonas was written in simple letters. There were 6 flowers following my name. I also saw 4 tallies. The pictures were similar to what I drew on my white loafers when I was in the Black and White Saloon. The music continued to play in a quieter mode now. Henley and I talked as the music played.

<u>I hear the drums echoing tonight</u>
<u>But she hears only whispers of some quiet conversation</u>
<u>She's coming in, 12:30 flight</u>

<u>The moonlit wings reflect the stars that guide me towards salvation</u>
<u>I stopped an old man along the way</u>
<u>Hoping to find some old forgotten words or ancient melodies</u>
<u>He turned to me as if to say</u>
<u>"Hurry boy, it's waiting there for you"</u>

    I have to admit I was happy to see someone I knew. It made me feel a little calmer to see Henley. I always thought he was a nice guy.

    "How long have you been here?" I asked Henley.

    "I have kind of lost track of time. I think I have been here for about a week." He said.

    "Aren't your parents wondering where you are? How long do we need to stay here? How do we get home?" I said in worry.

    Henley then started loudly singing the chorus to Africa. I danced and he sang.

<u>It's gonna take a lot to drag me away from you</u>
<u>There's nothing that a hundred men or more could ever do</u>
<u>I bless the rains down in Africa</u>
<u>Gonna take some time to do the things we never had (ooh, ooh)</u>

    We both started laughing about our awkward singing and dancing. We continued to discuss what was next as Toto played from above like elevator music.

doodle here

The Artist's Playlist

"We have to complete the OMNIFICLAND tasks and play the game to the end. I would think my parents would be worried about me too." Henley replied seriously.

He didn't seem to be stressed about it. He was very matter of fact about the whole deal. I noticed that he also had a white pair of loafers on his feet. He had 5 flowers on the right loafer and 5 tallies on the left loafer. He noticed me looking at his loafers and then he looked at mine.

"I like the flowers you drew on your shoe." Henley said this as he examined my loafer.

"Thanks! I see you have five daisies on your shoe." I replied.

I wondered how he answered the test questions. I wondered if he answered similar to mine.

"So, did you pick the black and white button when you went on the elevator?" I asked.

"Yes, I did. It just seemed like the most normal one to me. I feel like I havn't been here much longer than you. I got to the cave not too long ago. I have my mixed tape and was about to continue on and then I heard your song start to play. Another One Bites the Dust... nice song!" Henley said.

"I know, right!? I love Queen. Their songs are EPIC! Did your mixed tape tell you where you have to go next? And, how do I get mine?" I asked.

"Your list is on the wall right now. Walk over to the wall. It will walk you through what you need to do." He motioned me to walk in the direction I needed to go.

I walked on the lit-up floor to the wall that displayed my play list. The electronic voice told me to place both my hands on the wall. I carefully placed my hands on the wall, like I was giving it two high fives. I held them on the wall for about 5 seconds. Then the voice instructed me to follow the pattern on the floor with my feet and on the wall with my hands. After she directed me to do so, one of the songs on my play list started to blare through the cave. It was number 4 – Sweet Caroline by Neil Diamond. This song makes me think of my dad. Neil is his all-time favorite singer. I know all of his songs because of my dad.

The lights changed to RED. The orchestra was playing the intro. I got myself ready by getting in a good stance and getting my eyes ready to follow the lights. The floor started a pattern to tap for my feet as the first verse began. Neil sang, and I did my best to follow the lights. As I danced I thought of my dad. I thought of how much I love to dance. I thought THIS IS FUN! 5-6-7-8

<u>Where it began, I can't begin to knowing</u>
 I tapped my feet to the lights.
<u>But then I know it's growing strong</u>

I tapped the wall in with my hands.
Was in the spring
I brushed the wall in one big sweep from left to right to follow the lights like a rainbow.
And spring became the summer
I did a side step and jumped with the lights.
Who'd have believed you'd come along
I slapped the wall with both hands and did a pivot turn with the lights.

I was having so much fun at this point that Henley decided to join me. We danced and followed the motions of the lights with the rest of the song.

Hands, touching hands
Reaching out, touching me, touching you
Sweet Caroline
"BAH BAH BAH!" Henley and I both sang loudly.
Good times never seemed so good
"SO GOOD, SO GOOD, SO GOOD!"
We laughed and sang.
I've been inclined
To believe they never would
But now I

    Just then the lights went all green and stopped flashing.

Henley said, "Here is when the cassette pops out. Get ready!"

The cave wall made a calculating sound and a part of the wall opened and dropped out a cassette tape. The cassette was in a clear plastic case.

Again, you could see that my name was on it. There were also six flowers behind my name, just like my right shoe. The jacket of the cassette had my top ten songs listed. It also had a drawing (sketch) of me inside. You could see four tallies on the tape as well. I knew what cassette tapes looked like. My mom and dad had some at our house in storage. I always thought they were kind of fun. I never had my own cassette tape and I wasn't really sure how they worked. I am used to just playing my music from my iPad or phone. I put the cassette in my black and white bag. I wanted to make sure I didn't forget it. As I was putting the cassette away, Henley was exiting the music cave.

Henley shouted, "Iris, let's go!"

I hurried along to catch up with him. As we walked out of the cave, the green lights continued to dance to the song Sweet Caroline. I pulled out my journal. It was amazing! There was the play list and the roll of my dice. It was all documented there in my journal. I got out my polaroid, took a selfie of me and Henley with the flashing cave behind us. I now had another pic in my journal. I put my camera away again.

"So, what is next Henley?" I asked.

"I am not sure. When you rolled the three dice, what was your third dice?" he questioned.

"I had a notebook and pencil. What did you have?" I then questioned him.

"Same for me! That is our next place to visit, but what is it? Where is it? How do we get there?" he said in wonder.

We looked around the exit of the cave. Instead of a purple brick road, a green brick road continued. Instead of lilac trees there were many trees.

They were really cool looking trees. I had heard my mom talk about these trees before. They are weeping willow trees. I loved how the leaves drooped. We decided we better just follow the green bricks to see where it led us. As we walked the wind blew lightly and the birds sang.

"I just love these weeping willow trees. They are so pretty." I announced. I decided to take a quick picture of the beautiful green path of large, swaying Willow Trees. I had never seen anything like it before.

I noticed that there was a sign coming up ahead. Henley noticed it too.

"Look a sign!" he said in excitement.

We walked a little faster. As we got closer, we noticed that it looked like directions. It was a plain and simple sign that had Writing Whereabouts written on top of it. There was a little notebook and pencil drawing on the sign too. Maybe this would help us know what to do next. I thought about how I was very happy that Henley was here with me. It was nice to have another mind to get through these tasks. We can do this together, I thought.

The sign read…

You have a gift of writing if you are here. You must follow the weeping willows to Writing Whereabouts.
You have a writing task ahead of you. Check journals for Weeping Willows.
"I love writing stories and poems. I think I get that from my dad." I explained.

Writing Whereabouts
You have a gift of writing if you are here. You must follow the weeping willows to Writing Whereabouts. You have a writing task ahead of you. Check journals for weeping willows.

"I like writing too, but I like writing songs. I just love music. That is what got me in this place. I was tapping my pencil to the beat of a song I had been working on. I kind of get lost in my own music world when I start thinking about writing songs. Mrs. Pepper asked me stop the other day. I didn't really hear her because I was so into my music. She then got my attention and gave me the OMNIFICLAND card. I had to go to the office and, well, you know what happened next." he described.

THE WEEPING WILLOWS

    We continued on our way to Writing Whereabouts by following the green Weeping Willow path. I wondered how long we would have to walk. These trees were not like typical weeping willows. As I walked with Henley, we began to hear faint crying. It sounded like crying puppies. Were there puppies nearby in trouble? Henley and I looked at each other wondering what it was. We walked closer to the noise. We stepped onto the grass that seemed like football turf. As we walked across this almost perfect grass, we got closer to the weeping willows. Once we were up close to the trees, we could see that they were crying or weeping. I also noticed that the leaves had words written on them. I guess that makes sense since we are on our way to Writing Whereabouts.

    Henley got out his OMNIFICLAND journal. He was frantically turning the pages.

    "What are you looking for?" I asked

    "Your journal is a guide as well. Get your journal out and look up Weeping Willows." he directed me.

    I got my OMNIFICLAND journal out of my bag. I was almost sure that there were just blank pages like a journal that added pictures from the magical polaroid camera. I opened the journal and realized that Henley was correct. This was a journal and guide. I opened up to the back, wondering if it had an index. There it was... OMNIFICLAND INDEX. I ran my finger over the page to find the words _weeping willows_. There it was. It directed me to page 44. I turned to the page and saw a picture of the tree, a definition and also some advice.

WEEPING WILLOW: *a Eurasian willow with trailing branches and foliage reaching down to the ground, widely grown as an ornamental in waterside settings. This willow is known to cry or weep when they see talent or creative people. The waterside holds their tears. Their leaves will give you advice and/or messages to lead you to your innermost/outermost creativity or omnificent truth*

When you come across a weeping willow and it is weeping, do the following things in this order…

1. *Walk around the trunk of the tree twice. As you walk sing or hum the 3rd song on your artist mix tape play list.*
2. *Continue the song after circling the tree. Look at the ground – pick up 7 leaves that have fallen to the ground. Pick them up quickly and do not look at them.*

3. Then carefully pick a branch that is hanging. Take seven more leaves off of the branch that is hanging. Again, you should not look at the words on the leaves while you pick and you should continue singing the 3rd song on your play list.
4. Once you have sung through the chorus, put your leaves in your bag. They will be safe until you get to Writing Whereabouts.

*** Note: If a Weeping Willow tree sees true talent in you, it weeps. If you are an extraordinary talent the leaves will turn colors. If you feel a Weeping Willow calling you, know that it is pure and its message is asking you to recognize all of the emotions that you feel. It is not good to keep feelings locked up. They should not go unnoticed. You can find your true feelings and passions with the Weeping Willow.

***Note: The Weeping Willow helps you find PURPOSE. Purpose is discovering what gives our lives meaning.
Willow trees show the way to survive turbulent times. They stand tall, are willing to bend so as not to break with the winds of change. They trust their own strength and resilience.

***Note: Willow Tree Leaves show us how beautiful change can be. We allow joy, sadness, happiness and pain to cycle with in us. We get peace by letting go, just like leaves.

Henley said he would go first. Which was fine with me. I have always been a little shy about singing. I was hoping some of his confidence would rub off on me. I was curious to see what Henley's 3rd song on his artist mix tape would be. He walked up to the tree we were closest to. He started to walk around the tree. He started to sing.

"S… A….F….E…. T…. Y….
SAFETY DANCE….
You can dance if you want to.

He circled the tree.

We can leave your friends behind

He had a bit of a beat in him as he walked. It was obvious he had rhythm and liked to dance.

'Cause your friends don't dance
And if they don't dance
Well, they're no friends of mine

His voice was pretty good.

Say, we can go where we want to
A place where they will never find
I knew this song. David Bowie!

And we can act like we come

I love this song! Men Without Hats is the name of the group that sings it. Classic 80s!

From out of this world
Leave the real one far behind

The leaves turned a baby blue as he sang.

And we can dance Or sing
We can go when we want to

After circling the tree, he picked 7 leaves off the ground. He then picked 7 blue leaves from a tree limb that was hanging.

Night is young and so am I
And we can dress real neat
From our hats to our feet
And surprise 'em with the victory cry

Say, we can act if we want to
If we don't, nobody will
And you can act real rude and totally removed
And I can act like an imbecile
And say, we can dance, we can dance

He continued to circle it and sing until he finished the chorus.

Everything's out of control
We can dance, we can dance
They're doing it from pole to pole

After his last time around he broke out into dance. And he could dance!

We can dance, we can dance
Everybody look at your hands

The Weeping Willow was keeping the beat for him. It was creating music.

We can dance, we can dance
Everybody's taking the chance

It was fun to watch. I smiled and tapped my own feet.

Safety dance

    Henley looked at me and smiled. He motioned to me and said, "Your turn!"
    I was a little nervous. I hadn't really sung in front of anyone before. I had danced for people many times. That was my strength musically. I said to myself more than anyone... "Here goes."
    I started to circle the tree. I touched the smooth bark with my fingers. It felt like I was under a big umbrella of leaves. It was amazing. I started to sing.

"Just a small-town girl

Henley looked surprised as I started to sing. I kept singing.

Livin' in a lonely world
She took the midnight train goin' anywhere
Just a city boy
Born and raised in south Detroit

The tree felt magical.

He took the midnight train goin' anywhere

A singer in a smoky room
All of a sudden, the tree turned colors. It was a beautiful bubble gum pink. My favorite color!

A smell of wine and cheap perfume
For a smile they can share the night
It goes on and on, and on, and on

I could almost smell bubble gum too. After going around once, I picked 7 leaves from the ground.

Strangers waiting
Up and down the boulevard
Their shadows searching in the night
Streetlights, people

I then picked 7 of the pink leaves from a drooping branch. I sang through the chorus under the vibrant pink leaves

Living just to find emotion   *Hiding somewhere in the night*

    It felt good to sing like that. I loved the feeling of expressing my feelings through song. Just like it said in the journal... It is not good to keep feelings locked up. Feelings were meant to be expressed. Does this have something to do with my purpose?

"Wow... You have an amazing voice! I mean wow!" said Henley.

"Thanks! You were amazing with your song too!

I took out my polaroid camera and took a picture under all the bubble gum pink leaves. I thought, I will NEVER forget this.

Should we see if we can figure out what we need to do next. Let's look at our leaves." I suggested.

"Here, let's go over here." He said. There was a clearing just by the trees. We sat down on the perfect-like turf. I got out my leaves while Henley got his out.

doodle here

Writing Whereabouts Words

Henley and I both laid out our leaves on the turf grass. We each had 14 leaves. As I was spreading out my leaves, I was saying them in my head. 7 of my leaves were green, and 7 were pink. I guess the leaves I picked up from the ground were green. The pink ones I picked from the tree while I was singing. The words I read in my mind were...

Green Leaves
acceptance
creativity
kindness
compassion
courage
growth
mindfulness

Pink Leaves
write
draw
sew
dance
create
help
lead

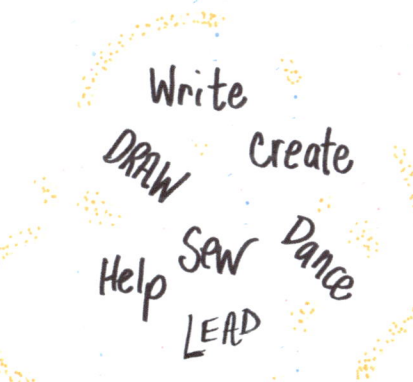

I wasn't sure if these words were supposed to be my strengths or weaknesses. I know that I really like doing the things on the pink leaves. The only one that made me squirm a little was the word lead.

I have never really seen myself as a leader. The other pink leaves were big passions of mine. How did the tree know? Was it because of my singing? The green leaves were maybe things I could work on. I wasn't quite sure how these words would help me or what I was supposed to do with them.

Henley was spreading his leaves out and reading them as well.

Green Leaves	**Blue Leaves**
Fun	write
creativity	drum
kindness	paint
generosity	dance
love	create
growth	help
musical	lead

Henley agreed that he felt like his blue leaves were his strengths, except for the word lead. Maybe there was a reason Henley and I were going through this together.

Maybe we both need to be leaders in our strengths. As we were looking at our leaves and trying to figure out what to do next, we heard a carriage with horses getting closer. This just kept getting more interesting. There was a person controlling the horses. The horses were green! GREEN! The horse hair was white and glittery. I had never seen green horses before. The carriage and horses stopped near us.

The carriage was full of silver glitter. I couldn't believe how it sparkled. It was almost like a disco ball. It shimmered in the sunlight.

Just then a fairy-like creature stepped out of the carriage, and partly walked and flew over to us. It was obvious the fairy creature was a girl. She had long hair, she was covered in glitter and she carried a star wand.

"Weeping Willows are so magical! Don't you just love them?" she said She glanced at the trees. She saw that one had turned blue and one was pink.

"Who are you?" asked Henley. He looked at her in a cautious way. He wasn't sure what to think of her yet.

"Hello, are you here to help us?" I asked.

"Hello dear humans. Henley and Iris." She said our names and looked at us as though she knew us.

"Hello," We both replied.

"I am here to guide you, but you must lead your own path. I am Farrah the Phrase Fairy" As she said this, glitter sprinkled out of her star wand. She flew around and hummed a tune. "Don't you just love words?" She yelled.

"I do love words! I love creating stories and poems... just like my dad." I said.

She stopped flying around and came close to us again. "You are about to complete the Epic Poetry Puzzle." She asked us to get out our OMNIFICLAND journals.

We got out our journals. She asked us to hold them in front of us, and to keep them closed. She took her wand and waved it above them. She said, "Words are the power, you will know within the hour." She then hit the journals with the wand. Glitter sprinkled them and the journals started to shine like a light. The light lasted for about 5 seconds and then faded.

Farrah the Phrase Fairy started to fly towards her carriage and wished us "word" luck.

"Wait! What are we supposed to do?" I shouted.

"Look in your journals!" she sang to us.

She got in the carriage and the horses trotted away. Glitter followed them as they vanished out of sight.

Ok! I guess the answer as to what was next is in the journals. We opened to journals to see what to do. They were now full of glitter, as we opened them. The words that were on the leaves, were now in the journals. There was a set of directions for the "EPIC POETRY PUZZLE".

EPIC POETRY PUZZLE RULES

Create a poem with several stanzas. You must include every word from your leaves.
It does not have to rhyme, but it must be true to your goals and dreams. Be honest with your feelings and beliefs. Follow the Painted Rock River to Share the poem with the Painted Dogs. Dogs can tell when you are showing your truth. They will let you know if you pass the test.

This was a challenge that sounded like fun to me. I rock at poetry. Plus, we get to see dogs! I LOVE DOGS! Henley was excited too. We decided to work on our poems separately and then share them with each other before we started the journey down the Painted Rock River.

We worked on the poems for quite some time under the Weeping Willow trees. We actually finished at about the same time. We came together and sat crisscross and faced each other. We both seemed a bit nervous to share our creations. I offered to go first. I explained that I chose to make my poem rhyme because that is what I am used to doing with poems. I told Henley that I really tried my best and that I thought it was true. Henley took the journal from my hands and said, "just give it to me."

He read the poem in silence and smiled a few times as he read it.

> To **dance** is to share your **creativity** with motion
> **Mindfulness** allows me to feel calm from all the commotion
> I long for **acceptance** when I **create** and **draw**
> I feel deep emotion and **kindness** when I dance because it is so raw
> I like to **sew** and **write** with all my soul
> I want to **help** and **lead**, but sometimes I don't sense it is my role
> I have the **compassion** and **courage** to grow,
> but sometimes that **growth** is just hard, you know

Henley looked up after reading my poem. He said, "It is very good! I really like it. I think it is very much YOU! Great job Iris!

"Thanks Henley! Can I ask you what your favorite part was? I am just curious." I said hesitantly.

"Iris, you need to believe in your words, because they are true! I really like how you talked about wanting to grow, but it is hard to do." He admitted.

"Thanks Henley. Well, I really want to read yours now." I said.

"Okay, well just so you know... mine doesn't rhyme. I mean I think it is okay." He stuttered.

I grabbed his journal and started to read. As I read I could almost hear Henley singing/rapping the poem. It was definitely matching his personality.

> I **love** to rhyme and play my **drum**
> It makes me **dance** and it's so much **fun**
> **Creativity** can come with **painting** or **writing**
> I spread **kindness** and **love** while I'm stomping
> I am so **musical**, I just can't **help** it
> **Creativity** starts in the heart and I feel it
> **Generosity** is something I find charming
> My **growth** will come when I **lead** my friends, oh yeah!

"I love it Henley!" I told him.

"Really? Do you really?" he said.

"Yes! Let's find the Painted Rock River. We are ready!" I said

"Let's find those painted puppies!" Henley laughed.

We started walking past the Weeping Willows. There was a small hill that lead down to a very colorful river. It was so amazingly pretty. I had never seen a river so bright. There was little water in the river. It was mainly painted rocks. I bent down to look at the rocks up close. I put my hand in the warm water. I grabbed a rock from the river. I looked at it sitting in my hand. It was bright yellow with a smiley face on it. I smiled.

"Hey Iris, I just looked up Painted Rock River in our journal. It says here that the rocks in the river are "kindness rocks". It says take what you need and pass on to people who may need some kindness. I was thinking I should take a few rocks with me. You never know when you will need to spread kindness. I took the I took the yellow smiley rock. I then grabbed a rainbow one that said *Be Your BEST You*! I love that!

"Look Henley! There is a giant rock over here. There is something written on it." I said.

The Giant rock was about as tall as my shoulders. There were etched words in it. There were paint brush strokes in all directions with several colors. It reminded me of a gravestone but it was very colorful. There was a quote on the rock as well as a dedication. It said...

Randy Rawls Rocks River
This rock river is in dedication to a man
who shared his love of painting to everyone.

Swish up, down and around.

"This Randy sounds like a pretty cool guy. I bet he really helped people. Wouldn't it be fun to paint rocks like these!" Henley inquired.

    I decided to see if there was anything in the OMNIFICLAND journal about Randy Rawls. I opened to the index. Sure enough there was information about him on page 55.

Randy Rawls

Randy Rawls lived a full life of creativity.
He cared deeply for his family.
He had two daughters and four grandchildren.
He was known for his beautiful, life-like portraits.
He tried to teach his daughters and grandchildren how important it is to express your creative side.
One of his famous quotes was…

> When your brush swishes up, the sun shines bright. When your brush swishes down, you feel like you are doing something right. Because when you swish any way, you are making someone's day.
> Swish up, down, and all around.
> *Randy Rawls*

Henley took a few of the rocks, but I didn't get to see which ones he took. After putting the rocks in our bags, we followed the river by walking along next to it. It felt as though the river would go on forever. At least we had a pretty view as we walked along the colorful rocks.

doodle here

The Painted Dogs

    After walking for quite a while, we started to hear some barking. There was a building in the distance. It was a black building with color splotches all over it. As we got closer, we noticed a sign in front of the building. It said... Painted Dog House. We walked up to the door and knocked. There was a sign that said DO NOT ring the doorbell. We waited patiently at the door. We heard barking inside. The building was very unique. There were no windows.

    A very short man answered the door. He was very athletic and quick. I guess he might need to be to keep up with a bunch of dogs. He was wearing a brown suit with orange accents. There was an orange hat, handkerchief, shoes and bow tie. He was quite fashionable.

    "Hello! My name is Winslow Coolidge! I am the king of the painted dogs. This is the Painted Dog House. My dogs are smart. They are colorful. They can read people. They can read your destiny." He said dramatically.

    "We were sent here by Farrah the Phrase Fairy. She said that we need to share our poems with the painted dogs." I said in an unsure way.

    "Come in! Please DO NOT look at the dogs. Keep your eyes up. You cannot look at them until you read your poems. They get very excited, but if you ignore... they will behave. Do your best to just follow me. No looking down." Demanded Winslow.

As we walked in, I noticed that there *were* windows. It was as though there were no walls. It looked as though we were outside. It must be some kind of magical painted walls. When we were outside, you couldn't see inside at all. I bet that is why the dogs were barking when we were getting close to the building. As we walked through the building the dogs were trying to get our attention. They were sniffing us and whining like most dogs do when there are visitors.

We followed Winslow to a back room. It looked like a theater. It had a stage and several comfy chairs, couches and bean bags facing the stage. Winslow walked up the stairs and lead us to the stage. As we went on the stage, the painted dogs went to the comfy chairs and sat down. As soon as they sat down, the room was silent. They stopped barking. It was as though they knew we were about to read our poems and they had to be quiet to listen.

Winslow turned to face us. His back to the audience (dogs).

"You will take turns and step up to the microphone. It is your job to read your poem. Say it with feeling and expression. If your poem is from the heart. If you succeed... the dogs will howl and change colors. This is their way of saying that they approve and feel your compassion." Winslow instructed.

"Are you ready?" Winslow asked as though he was a ringmaster at a circus.

Henley and I both answered yes at the same time. We then looked at each other nervously and smiled.

"Henley, you go first." Winslow insisted.

"You got this Henley!" I encouraged him.

We hadn't really looked at the dogs yet. I guess they were trained to stay at their seats for the poem readings. It was funny how they all sat there. It was as though they were about to watch a movie or something. I think they knew that they had an important job to do for us.

Henley stepped up to the microphone. He opened his OMNIFICLAND journal to the poem. He cleared his throat and started to stomp his foot to a beat. He read his poem just as I imagined it when I read it silently by the Painted Rock River.

> I love to rhyme and play my **drum**
> It makes me **dance** and it's so much **fun**
> **Creativity** can come with **painting** or **writing**
> I spread **kindness** and **love** while I'm stomping
> I am so **musical**, I just can't **help** it
> **Creativity** starts in the heart and I feel it
> **Generosity** is something I find charming
> My **growth** will come when I **lead** my friends, oh yeah!

After half rapping, half speaking his poem, he looked up and noticed the dogs were wagging their tails. The dogs started to howl and changed all different colors. It was like when Christmas lights change color, except it was like paint changing colors on the dogs. Henley smiled and took a big sigh. I think he was glad it was over and the dogs approved.

Winslow smiled and dramatically announced, "The painted dogs approve!"

I began to get nervous. What if the dogs don't approve of my poem?

"Your turn Iris! Get ready!" Winslow motioned for me to step up to the microphone.

I slowly took three steps up to the microphone. I decided to hold the microphone in my hand. I sat on the floor of the stage and opened up my journal. I looked up and saw all the dogs staring at me. I took a deep breath and started to speak clearly and I did my best to speak from my heart.

> To **dance** is to share your **creativity** with motion
> **Mindfulness** allows me to feel calm from all the commotion
> I long for **acceptance** when I **create** and **draw**
> I feel deep emotion and **kindness** when I dance because it is so raw
> I like to **sew** and **write** with all my soul
> I want to **help** and **lead**, but sometimes I don't sense it is my role
> I have the **compassion** and **courage** to grow,
> but sometimes that **growth** is just hard, you know

I got emotional as I spoke. I really did feel what I was reading. As I finished reading, I heard silence. A single golden retriever walked up the stage and sat next to me. He put his head in my lap and started to whine. All the dogs started howling and the room filled with colorful painted dogs again. The dog that had come on stage started kissing my cheek. I smiled and pet his head.

    Winslow started to clap. "Oh my dogs! Rizzo really likes you. He has seen your true inner beauty. Rizzo, come here!"

    Rizzo ran over to Winslow and jumped in his arms. He was a very energetic dog with a positive feel to him.

    "The painted dogs approve again! I have never seen Rizzo do that to anyone! You have really expressed your compassion! Great job to both of you!" Winslow said with Rizzo still in his arms. He was impressed.

    "If only Mrs. Pepper could see me now. She would've loved our poems, Henley!" I announced.

    "Well, I don't know who Mrs. Pepper is... but she should be happy to know that you two have passed the test. You are on your way to Integrity Island! Your poems were superb... amazing... and worth listening to." Said Winslow.

    "So, how do we get to this Integrity Island?" asked Henley

    "Is it actually an Island?" I asked.

    "It is an island of flowers. ANY kind of flower you can think of. Flowers Farm has magical, flying creatures there. You will continue together to this island and find the Hill of Zinnias. Here you will get advice from a flying friend. The painted dogs and I wish you luck. Remember to be kind and show self-love always. We will not forget you... Right Rizzo?" Winslow said to the dog Rizzo. Rizzo barked in agreeance.

"Wait, Winslow... Can we take a picture with you and the painted dogs?" I pleaded.

"Of course! Painted dogs! Come, sit and smile at the camera!" He invited the dogs to the stage.

I was excited to take such a fun picture. I will always remember this place of the painted dogs. I did my best to hold up the polaroid camera to take a selfie. I was hoping it would turn out.

"Everybody say cheese!" I said smiling.

We got the picture. I put my camera away, along with my OMNIFICLAND journal. Winslow Coolidge pointed us in the direction we needed to go. We continued on a path that was similar to the Weeping Willows, except there were no trees. The path was green brick. Winslow told us to walk the green path until we came across a field that leads to a farm. We will need to stop at the farm for directions to Integrity Island. You will need to create something on the farm before you continue.

The Blue Dasher Dragonflies

As we walked, we talked about how awesome our poems turned out. Those painted dogs were so awesome. I love how they would change all different colors. They were just so bright and friendly.

"That is one thing I have always loved about dogs. They love you no matter what. They really have true compassion." Said Henley.

All of a sudden, we came across a beautiful field of corn. It was truly special how the corn stood strong in perfect rows. Whomever planted this corn knew exactly what they were doing. This field was almost a piece of art. Along the field of corn was a gravel road. There was a sign that said, This way to Zinnia Hill.

"There!" I pointed.

"Yes! Great job Iris. Let's go." Henley agreed.

We continued on and walked along the gravel road. Walking here made me think of my grandparent's farm. I always love visiting there. Just ahead there was a small grove of trees. I saw a farm house, large farm garage and a fenced in area with some horses. There was a man and a woman on the road next to the house. They looked very friendly. The man was wearing worn out overalls and a farmer hat. The woman had a farm dress on. It was almost as though they stepped out of a Laura Ingalls Wilder book. As we walked the gravel road and got closer to them, they started walking towards us. Once we were in talking distance the woman introduced herself.

"Hello my dears. My name is Betty. This is Smokey, my husband. Winslow told us you were coming. Are you Iris and Henley?" She asked.

"Yes, we are! It is nice to meet you both. Your farm is very nice. Can you help us find Zinnia Hill?" asked Henley.

"We will help you get to Zinnia Hill, but why don't you come in for a bite to eat first. You must be famished after all your traveling." said Betty

"I guess we could do that, right Iris?" replied Henley

I agreed that it would be a good idea to get a bite, plus I needed to use the restroom. We walked up the path to the farm house. As we walked, I thought about how I was just in Mrs. Pepper's class not too long ago. Now I was at a farm after talking to an oversized Sharpie, traveled down a purple path, danced in a musical cave, talked to weeping willows, followed a rock river to the painted dogs and now I was on a farm. Will I ever get back to my classroom? How many more places will I visit? I also thought of The Eraser that Sharpay told me about. I really hope I don't run into him. I was lost in my thoughts when all of a sudden, I realized there were several little farm kittens at my feet. Betty told me not to mind them. They always go to visitors.

Henley and I followed the couple into their matter of fact farm home. It made me think of the family farm I often visit on holidays. I wondered if they had a big family like mine. We walked into a kitchen/dining area. Henley and I sat down at an oval kitchen table. Smokey sat with us. Betty went to the kitchen to get some warm homemade butter biscuits. They smelt so good. She brought the basket of biscuits over with some honey and butter. I had to admit that I was so hungry. It had to be lunch time by now. I had been gone for what seemed like forever.

Henley and I ate biscuits and drank fresh lemonade with this lovely farm couple. It was a nice little break from all our travels. It was the first normal thing that really happened so far in OMNIFICLAND. After eating, we took turns using the restroom and decided to head on our way. Betty walked us past the tree grove and explained what road to take to the Zinnia Hill.

As we walked along up a gravel hill Henley and I talked about how good the biscuits were that we just ate. It seemed as though the hill kept on going up, and finally we reached the top. When we stopped at the top of the hill, we looked at each other in awe. The land ahead was COVERED in color. Hills of zinnias went on for as far as we could see! There was any color you could think of. There were several bugs of some kind flying all around the flowers and in the air. What were they?

"Look! What are those? I wonder if these are the flying creatures that Winslow was talking about?" asked Henley

"They look like giant dragon flies, don't they?" I responded.

I wondered if they would harm us or if they were friendly. I couldn't believe how big they were. We were still quite a ways from them but I was a little nervous to get closer.

"Hey! I know what these are! They are Blue Dasher Dragonflies. Yes! I had to do research on these guys for my cub scouts project. They are very common and widely spread through North America and into the Bahamas." Henley informed me.

He continued, "Although the species name means "long wings", their wings are not substantially longer than those of related species. The males are easy to recognize because of their vibrant blue color, yellow-striped thorax, and metallic green eyes. They develop a frost color with age." Henley shared excitedly.

"Wow, I am impressed Henley. I think you are right. They do look like dragon flies. The color of them is amazing. They are so pretty!" I said.

I wondered if there was something about these dragonflies in our OMNIFICLAND journal. I took out my journal and looked in the index again. There it was... Blue Dasher Dragonflies!

Blue Dasher Dragonfly

Having flown the earth for 300 million years, dragonflies symbolize our ability to overcome times of hardship. They remind us to take time to reconnect with our own strength, courage and happiness. The Blue Dasher Dragonfly is a symbol of transformation and transcendence. It represents the journey from darkness into light, the afterlife and the freedom of the spirit.

The dragonfly is the keeper of dreams. They inspire creativity. They remind us that anything is possible.

If you happen to run into a Blue Dasher Dragonfly do the following…

1. Call the dragonflies by chanting a word that makes you happy. Hold your arm out to the side. Chant the word over and over until the dragonfly lands on your arm. Make sure to really think about the thing that makes you happy.
2. Once the dragonfly lands on your arm, look at him with a smile.
3. Make a wish and whisper it to the dragonfly.
4. Once the dragonfly hears your wish, it will fly away with your happiness and your wish. It will do its best to make your dreams come true.

"Now this sounds fun! I want to go first. Is that ok?" asked Henley.
"Yes, Mr. Dragon fly expert… you go first. Ok… start chanting a word that makes you happy. Oh, but wait. Do you have a wish ready?" I asked Henley. Trying to get him prepared.

"Yes, and Yes! Ok, here I go. *Dance, dance, dance, dance, dance, dance.*" Henley began to chant his word.

As he chanted the word dance, I watched the dragon flies. While he said the word over and over the dragon flies flew quickly through the air. I wondered how long he would have to chant. Just as I was thinking this, a huge dragon fly started to swoop down and fly towards us. It was swaying in an awkward pattern. As it got closer we realized how big it really was. Henley held out his arm. The large insect flew around his arm a few times and then landed around the inside of his elbow. It was HUGE! It was about the size of a pheasant. I looked at the dragon fly. It was so amazingly bright and unique. The wings were shiny and glistened in the sunlight. The dragon fly was looking at Henley. Henley looked intently at the giant insect. He leaned his head closer to it. He whispered his wish to the dragonfly. The dragonfly looked at him and then at me. He swooped down and up and around both of us. Then it flew away quickly. I didn't hear what his wish was but I figured it would be bad luck to share it.

I started to chant my word. I looked at the sky and said the word *create* over and over. I know that creating makes me happy. It is what gives me pure joy. I think of my family and how much I love all the ways they *create*. I knew *create* would be the word to chant. As I chanted, I looked up to see a dragon fly coming towards me. I nervously held out my arm.

All of a sudden, I felt the weight of an object on my arm. It almost seemed like a bird had landed on me. I looked the dragon fly in the eyes. I leaned a little closer to the dragon fly and whispered my wish. The dragon fly nodded at me and flew away. I watched him fly until I couldn't see him anymore. I couldn't believe that just happened. If you asked me this morning if I would ever see a giant blue dasher dragon fly up close and in person, I would say that it would never happen. Today had definitely taken a crazy twist on my normal days. I was excited to see that Henley took a picture of the dragon fly on my arm. I wish I would have thought to do that for him. What a cool memory to have in a picture. I opened my OMNIFICLAND journal and saw the picture. The dragon fly was so unique and colorful.

    I wondered if our wishes would come true. It seemed a bit far-fetched that a wish could happen because you whispered it to a Blue Dasher Dragon Fly. I guess we would have to wait and see.

10

Paintbrush Forest

After our amazing experience with the Blue Dashers, we weren't quite sure what to do next. We made our wishes and now we were wondering where our path would take us now. I thought about home. I knew we wouldn't be in this place forever, but how were we going to get back? Is there something we were missing?

"Well, I am not sure what we are supposed to do next." Henley announced.

I guess Henley was thinking the same thing. I looked at him and nodded. Just as we were both thinking about what the possible next step would be, we started to hear this odd noise. It sounds familiar, but I couldn't think of what it was.

"What is that?" I asked Henley.

Henley looked up and slightly ducked. "I am not sure?" he replied.

We were both really nervous about the sound we were hearing. Just then we started to see bright colors appearing in the sky. We heard the sound again. SWisHHHH… SwiSHHHHHH … SWISSHHHHHH. The sound was getting louder.

SWisHHHH... SwiSHHHHHH ... SWISSHHHHHH.

    The color in the sky was unbelievable. We followed the color and the noise. It must be something that we should see and follow. As we followed the sound we noticed a forest ahead. This was not like your typical forest. The trees were actually as tall as sequoias, but they were paintbrushes.

    The tops of the trees/paintbrushes were all different colors. It is like they were used to paint some colorful masterpiece. Again, I was amazed at how this trip was turning out. How could it be that I was just in a field of giant dragon flies and now I am in a forest made of vibrant paintbrushes.

    "Iris, can you believe this? I think that noise is someone painting. Doesn't it sound like paintbrushes painting?" Henley asked.

    "What should we do Henley? I am feeling really unsure and nervous about this." I said nervously.

    Henley looked at me. He was unsure what to say and I could tell that he felt nervous too. I thought now would be a good time for me to show that I could be a leader and show that I could be strong. I suggested that we should keep walking through this paintbrush forest. I felt that an answer was near. We walked slowly and continued to follow the sound. As we walked I started to hear a faint voice.

    "You are so talented Iris. I believe in you and I know you can do this." Said a familiar voice. "You are also talented Henley. I know you can do this too!"

    "I know that voice! It is Mrs. Pepper!" exclaimed Henley.

    "Yes! I knew I knew that voice! Is she here?" I asked.

I didn't see her anywhere, but we both heard her. We followed her voice. It led us to a painting. The painting was beautiful. It was a painting of a book with an apple. It was nicely done. At the bottom of the painting it said Joyce Pepper. I did not realize that Mrs. Pepper's first name was Joyce. As I looked at the painting, it made me think of something. It was familiar for some reason. It made me feel at home and I had a recognizable feeling.

Just then Henley screamed something. He said, "The hallway of art! You know the LONG hallway of art at school!!!"

"YES! I yelled.

That is why it is familiar. The frame was the same as all the paintings that were framed in that long beautiful art hallway at school. Had Mrs. Pepper been to OMNIFICLAND? There were two paintbrush trees just past Mrs. Pepper's painting. They had blank framed canvases on them. Each canvas was surrounded my several paintbrushes. They were just floating in the air, as if they were begging to be used.

"I think we need to paint!" said Henley.

I think Henley was right. We walked up to the canvases. We each stood in front of a canvas. As soon as we did this, the trees began to talk. Paint a picture both from your past, present and future. Combine each time into one piece of art. Be creative and colorful. Once you have completed the painting, sign your name in the bottom right hand corner.

"Do you realize what is happening Henley? We get to create art! I feel like these pieces of art might somehow appear in that long hallway of art at school." I excitedly explained.

"This is important Iris. We need to really create some masterpieces here. I love how the brushes float in the air. How do they not drip?" Henley asked.

"We better get started. Maybe this painting will help us get back to school." I stated.

I began to think about what I wanted to paint. It had to be from my past, present and future. I had to do something exceptional. Well I felt like I had to include my amazing artistic family in some way. I think I would somehow picture my family members and how they have taught me to be artistic. As for the present, I think I would include my school and important adults who have helped me. And for my future, I think I will somehow show me being an artist. It is what I love. Okay, now that I had my ideas, I had to combine them somehow. I looked over at Henley. He was behind me, and he was already creating. I wondered what he was painting. He was using a lot of different color brushed. He would grab one and paint. Then throw that brush in the air and grab another. It was crazy how they just floated.

I knew what to do. I had the perfect idea, but it would take some time. I got right to work. I painted and it was much easier than I thought it would be. Henley and I were having a lot of fun creating. As we created you could hear the loud paintbrush sounds. I was getting close to done and

I think Henley was too, when all of a sudden, the ground shook. I stopped painting and looked at Henley. The shaking happened again. It was scary and it continued to happen. It was almost like a giant was walking towards us. BOOM! BOOM! BOOM!

"Henley, should we hide?" I asked him frantically.

"Come this way!" He shouted. He led me under one of the biggest paintbrush trees.

I was scared. Was this a giant or an earthquake? We started to see a figure appearing in the distance. It looked like a giant eraser with arms and legs. He looked mean.

"It's the ERASER!" I whispered.

"What?" Henley whispered. He was confused.

"Sharpay warned me about him. She said he shows up in times of doubt. Were you doubting yourself? Maybe I was showing doubt." I blabbered on and on.

"It will be ok. We just need to stand up to this ERASER. We can do that, Right?" He asked.

"I don't know, he is so big. What is I get scared?" I almost started to cry.

"We can do this." Henley said.

We walked out to the ERASER. We help hands and tried to look brave.

The ERASER stomped up to us. He looked mean. He spoke loud and said, "WHO DO YOU THINK YOU ARE? You are not artist. What kind of paintings are those!? You should just give up. You are not meant to paint!"

I took a deep breath. I said, "Who do you think you are? The painting police? We have worked hard on this art! You don't know us, and you shouldn't go around judging people like that. It is rude and mean! I think you should keep walking mister!"

The ERASER was surprised at how I spoke to him. He slowly knelt down and looked at our paintings. He started to cry and said, "I am sorry I was so mean. Your art work is beautiful. I really love what you have done here. I am sorry."

I walked up to the ERASER. I put my hand on his hand and said, "Love others and enjoy each others' talents. Compliment and show appreciation for everyone's version of art. Everyone sees things in their own way."

He said, "You are right Iris. I am so glad that you said that. What you have learned on your journey has earned you and Henley two tickets on the bus to get you closer to your school."

Henley and I smiled and jumped up and down. We were so excited to hopefully be heading in the right direction.

The ERASER handed us two tickets. He told us that we had to exit the Paintbrush Forest and head to the Wool Transit.

"You must visit one more place before heading back. There is a lesson that you must learn at a new location before you will head home." ERASER smiled.

We took the tickets and started to head in the direction ERASER told us. We looked at the tickets. We were on our way. I put them in my bag. As I put them in my bag, I got out my polaroid camera. I turned back around and yelled, "ERASER! Can we get a quick picture with you?"

ERASER was so excited! He smiled and said, "No one has ever asked me that before. I would love to get a picture."

I gave him the camera. He held out the camera and took a selfie of the three of us. He waved good bye to us and walked the other direction. After only walking a short distance, we saw a sign that said Wool Transit. We were on our way.

doodle here

The Wool Transit

The sign that we saw said 5 miles to Wool Transit. I knew that a transit was a way to travel somewhere. I wasn't quite sure why it said "wool" transit. I knew that wool comes from sheep. A lot of clothes are made of wool. Did this have something to do with cloth? I didn't know if I had the energy to walk five miles to the transit. Just as I was thinking this, I heard Henley yell.

"Check this out!" he sounded excited.

"What?" I said as I looked towards him.

Henley was standing next to some kind of large machine. I didn't see it before, but it was clear as day now. It was like a giant vending machine. As I walked up to it I noticed that there wasn't candy inside. It had motorized scooters. I was happy to see scooters, but could've went for the candy.

"I was standing here thinking I didn't want to walk anymore. I leaned against this paint brush tree and wished to myself. I wished we could get to the transit quickly. Just after I wished it, the paintbrush tree turned into this vending machine. It was like my wish came true." Henley said in shock.

We pushed the button on the vending machine and were able to grab the scooters. I was hoping I could wish for something too. Maybe it would work for me. After getting my scooter, I walked over to one of the paint brush trees. I put my hand on it and wished for a snack and some water. Just like that, another vending machine appeared. This time it had several bottles of water and some small bags of snacks.

"Alright! Nice thinking Iris. Let's put some of these in our bags." He said excitedly.

We pushed the button and stuffed our bags. We got on our scooters and started riding to the transit. These scooters were amazing. They were different than a normal scooter. There was a whole platform to stand on, instead of a small bar. I was able to easily place both feet on the board with plenty of room remaining. The handle bars were higher, so I didn't have to bend over. There was also a safety belt that immediately fastened when you stepped onto the platform. There was a GPS device. It asked me where I wanted to go. I stated that I wanted to go to the Wool Transit.

As soon as I told the scooter this, it counted down from 5 and began moving. Henley did the same thing with his scooter. I couldn't believe how smooth the ride was. I think we were probably traveling about 15 miles an hour. This should get us there in no time, I thought. I was happy that Henley was able to get the scooters. I was tired from this journey and had no energy. It was also nice to have the snacks and water to revive us.

The ride was nice. There was a cool breeze, the sun was shining and I could hear birds singing. It only took us about four minutes to get to the transit. As we pulled up to the transit, I saw a white bench and a sign that said Wool Transit. As we approached the scooters stopped on their own. Both scooters said, "Arrived at location, Wool Transit." They unbuckled us automatically and we stepped off of them. We saw a small sign next to the bench that stated the times the transit would come. They come every 15 minutes. We decided to sit on the bench and have a snack. I got out the water from my bag, and Henley got out the snacks.

This is exactly what I needed. The water was great, but the snacks were like nothing I had ever seen. The packaging read IMAGINATION CRAVINGS. I opened a bag of the snack. They were shaped like cheese balls but they were green. Henley had a bag as well. He opened a bag and threw two green snacks in his mouth.

"OH my gosh! These are so good. I wasn't sure what they would taste like. I was hungry for hot dogs. I was thinking about hot dogs with ketchup and mustard on them. They taste EXACTLY like that! It was like it read my mind? Is that possible? You try." Henley demanded.

I knew what sounded good to me. A big bowl of mac n cheese. I imagined the taste. I threw one of the snacks in my mouth.

"This is crazy! I imagined mac n cheese. It tastes exactly like mac n cheese! It must just taste like whatever you are craving. They are called IMAGINATION CRAVINGS. YUM!" I said satisfyingly.

We finished our snacks and had a refreshing drink. Just as we finished we heard a vehicle coming. Sure enough there was a bus coming our way. It looked like a normal school bus, but very colorful. The side of the bus said "Home is where the YARN is." It also said WOOL BUS #7.

As the bus stopped, the door opened. We heard a voice yell, "All inside will enjoy the ride!"

We looked at each other and stepped towards the bus. In the bus was a driver. She looked at us and waved hello. She was wearing a crocheted vest with felt covered buttons. She had fun jeans on with bright colored embroidery all over them. She had flowers, birds, butterflies and fun designs of every color you could think of. Her long hair was in braided pig tails. She reminded me of the seventies.

"Greetings there! Wool you be joining us?" She said with a giggle.

"Yes, we will." I said nervously.

"Get it, Wool you be joining us? You know the Wool Transit. Ha Ha! Hop on board" She said again giggling.

We slowly stepped onto the bus. What I saw as I stepped on what NOT at all what I thought. I was expecting to see a normal inside of a bus. This was like nothing I had ever seen before.

"Wow! This is amazing!" I said to the woman.

She was very sweet. She spoke in a soft and high-pitched voice. She made me feel comfortable and at ease. She smiled at us as we stepped on the bus. She got out of the driver's seat and followed us as we found a seat.

"Hi Iris and Henley. My name is Sara. I will be your driver today on the Wool bus #7. Feel free to find a seat that is comfortable for you. If you feel like creating on the trip, do so. We encourage creation and exploration of your imagination." Sara said happily.

I took a picture of the bus before we stepped inside. The inside of the bus was completely covered in felt, yarn and wool. I noticed a felted bird hanging from her rear-view mirror.

There were wool couches with crocheted blankets, and pillows. The walls were covered in felt and felted art work. There was SO much color! There were coffee tables set up between the couches. On the tables were baskets of yarn and tools to crochet or knit. I had never done either but I had felted before. I noticed there was Styrofoam, needles and batts of wool. This could be fun to do as we travel on this bus! I decided to take a few more pictures inside. I knew I would never see a bus like this again.

"Our trip will take us about 20 minutes. Please feel free to have fun creating or you could take a nap if you need one. We will be at the Quilter's Corner before you know it." Sara said before she went back up to the driver's seat.

Sara seemed to be one of the nicest people I had ever met. She was genuinely kind and understanding. I was so excited to hear that we were going to a place that had to do with quilts. I wished my mom was with me when I heard our destination. I bet it is an amazing place. A place my mom and grandma would appreciate.

"Wait, do we need to give you the tickets?" I said as I reached for them. I couldn't find them.

"Your tickets are scrapped in your OMNIFICLAND books. I knew you had tickets that moment you got them from the ERASER. No need for tickets. Off we go" Explained Sara.

Sara began to drive. I looked in my journal and sure enough, there they were. Then I thought about our paintings. We forgot to bring them.

"Henley, we forgot our paintings!" I said in disappointment.

"Oh man, I really liked what I created too. We can't go back though." Henley said.

I knew that he was right. We couldn't go back, but I was disappointed that I couldn't have my painting. I looked over at Henley and laughed as he was trying to knit and had no idea what he was doing. He laughed too when he realized he had no clue what he was doing.

I grabbed the felting tools and began to felt. I decided to make a garden of colorful flowers. I picked a blue piece of felt for my background. I picked several bright batts of wool to create the garden. I took the felting needle out of its case. I picked a pink piece of wool and started to stab the wool into the shape of flowers. I continued to create as we traveled. After a few minutes of creating, I looked over and saw Henley sound asleep. I have to admit that I was tired and could probably fall asleep. I was having way too much fun with this wool. After about 20 minutes, I had created an amazing garden of felt. I decided I would give it to Sara. She was just so nice and she was helping us get where we needed to go.

"Approaching Quilter's Corner, Approaching Quilter's Corner." Announced the bus voice.

Sara put the bus in park and opened the bus door. She stood up and said, "It has been a pleasure to be your driver today. I hope you enjoyed your ride! Please continue creating and caring for others." She said with a wave and a smile.

As we stepped off the bus, I gave Sara my small garden creation. She thanked me and I noticed her hanging it with all the other creations inside.

The bus drove off and a little cabin was now in view. The cabin was small and cozy. There was a sign right outside in the front yard. It said The Quilter's Corner. The cabin was decorated with many flowers in the front yard. I noticed zinnias, black-eyed susans, sweet pea, snap dragons and so many more flowers I could name.

There were several unique bird feeders hanging from trees and Sheppard's hooks. It was a passion of mine to watch birds. I just find them fascinating. As we walked closer I noticed gold finch, cardinals, chickadees, and even humming birds. I got out my polaroid camera and took some pictures of the birds and flowers. I knew my mom would love them.

I had a feeling that this place might end up being my favorite part of this amazing trip.

12 The Quilter's Message

We walked up the cobblestone path to the front door. The birds flew right up to us. I had never gotten so close to birds before. Suddenly a finch landed on my shoulder. It is like it was saying hello. It was so cute and so yellow.

"Did you see that?" I asked Henley.

"Yes! A cardinal just landed on my finger too! This was so amazing." Said Henley.

I could've just stayed in the front yard and played with the birds, but I thought we should continue on and see what this last stop was about. The front door was large and had a rounded top. There were stain glassed windows surrounding the sides of the door. It was all so unique and amazing.

There was not a doorbell, but there was an old-fashioned door knocker that looked like a woodpecker. When you knocked, it was as if the woodpecker was knocking. After knocking we heard footsteps. A small, old woman answered the door. She was wearing a blue shall and yellow wool pants. She had a pale pink blouse on and her hair was in a bun. She reminded me of Easter time.

"Come in dearies. I have been waiting for you. I know you have taken a long journey. Let's have a spot of tea before we start. Do you like Earl Grey tea with a pinch of ginger?" she said in her soft, old voice.

We followed her to her small, cottage kitchen. A whole wall in her kitchen was carpentered boxes to display about a hundred mugs she had. It really decorated the kitchen neatly. There were mugs of every size, color and shape. She had some fun mugs ready on the table to serve her tea. She poured the tea and then handed us each a mug. My mug was bigger like a bowl and got smaller on top. It said Cup of Sunshine on it. There was a sun with flowers all around. Henley got a mug that looked more like a stein and it had a fun looking dog on it. After pouring our drinks she put a plate of fresh cut lemons on the table.

"It is always good with a squeeze of lemon, try it." She suggested.

Henley and I both took a lemon and squeezed it into our mugs. I dropped my lemon in my mug and Henley set his on the table.

"I love to put the whole piece of lemon in my mug too. Well then, my name is Mable Stitcher. I am a quilter. I have been quilting since I was your age. My mother and grandmother taught me. It is my favorite thing to do." She said before taking a sip of her tea. "Do you like the tea?"

"It is very good. Thanks!" I said.

Henley nodded in agreement.

"Take a few more sips and then we will begin." She instructed.

She left her tea and motioned for us to follow her. She led us through her cute little house to a back room that seemed to be like a big fabric store.

"This is what I call the Fabric Bin." She pointed to the room we just walked in.

There were so many bolts of fabric. There were patterns, solids, and anything you could think of. If only my mom and grandma were with me. They would LOVE this.

I looked at Mable and said, "What are we supposed to do now?"

Mable looked at us and said, "You must pick out the fabric you want to make a quilt. Choose wisely. It is important to pick fabrics that you like and that fit your personality."

I wasn't sure how many fabrics to pick, but I just started picking the ones that caught my eye. I chose fabrics with flowers, dogs, paintbrushes, fun designs and some solid colors too. The fabrics did not fit together, but I figured that once they were a quilt, the picture would make sense. That is what my mom always said.

Henley picked mostly solid colors. He also found some fabric with boomboxes and sneakers. The fabric he picked was TOTALLY him.

After we picked out our fabrics, Mable took us to another room that was full of sewing machines and other machines I had never seen before. She showed us each to a machine we would be using. I wasn't sure how we would be able to get a quilt done in little time. My mom worked on quilts and sometimes it would take her months to get them completed.

Mable told us to not worry. She said there were several lessons to learn but it would be done in a short amount of time. I trusted what she said. She sure liked to talk. Henley and I just listened and nodded as she told us all the lessons you can get from quilting.

"The first lesson you will learn with quilting is patience. You must be patient with each step of the quilting process. It can be hard. You will make mistakes, and that is okay. Mistakes are good, and you can fix mistakes easily. Perfection is overrated! I am not aiming for a grand prize when I quilt. You must aim for joy. The joy the quilt brings you or whomever you are gifting it to. Color is also important. Quilts don't have to be "matchy - matchy". They can be vibrant and bright. Improvising is the last thing. You make choices to create your quilt. Sometimes you improvise to create the beauty. I am convinced that quilting keeps my brain working at top efficiency. Let's get started."

I put the fabrics I had picked in a neat pile. Henley did the same. As we were doing this, Mable left the room for a second. She came back in quickly and gave us each a square piece of metal. It looked like a cookie cutter. We looked at each other, not sure what to do.

She said, "This is a magical tool called a squigger that you will only find in OMNIFICLAND. If you tap your fabric pile with this tool. It will magically be cut into the sizes you need. Go on now, try it."

I was now understanding how we were going to quickly make a quilt, with magic. I took the tool and tapped my fabric pile. Magically my fabric was in a perfectly cut pile of fabric. I wish this could work at home. I don't know how many times I had watched my mom cut fabric. It was hard work. This tool made it easy.

After Henley and I both had our stacks of cut cloth, Mable left the room again. She came back in and motioned for us to come with her again. She said to bring our piles of cut fabric. We followed her to a large room with two large and square tables. We each went to our own table and she directed us to set down our piles of cut fabric. On each table there was a button. She assured us that this is not how you quilt but we had to get done quickly, so she had to use her magic tools. She directed us to press the button on the table when we were ready. Henley and I decided just by looking at each other to push the button at the same time.

When we pushed the button, the table started to shake and make a sewing machine type noise. The fabrics started to move to different places on the table until it formed a pattern and design. Before we knew it, the fabric was being sewn into an amazing quilt. I couldn't even understand how it was being done. Henley and I looked at each other in disbelief. I knew how much time and energy went into quilts. I knew that this was not realistic, but how cool to make a quilt in just minutes.

Mable walked around the tables to inspect the quilts as they were being sewn. After making a lap around the tables she stated, "Your quilts were created in your imagination. They should be exactly as you thought. Are they to your satisfaction?"

"I love mine so much, it is exactly how I pictured it. It is amazing!" Said Henley.

"Mine too. It is like the machine read my mind." I said.

"A true quilt maker makes quilts for others. They make them to share love and it is an amazing love. You can wrap the love around you whenever you need it." Explained Mable.

Just as she was explaining this to us, birds flew in and picked up our quilts. We were able to see the whole quilt and their amazing designs. The birds then folded them into a neat pile. Mable advised us to pick them up. We picked them up and she told us to give them as a gift when we saw fit. We put the quilts in our bags to keep them safe. Mable told us to share them with love.

"You will be ready to move on. You are closer to home my dearies." Mable said.

I asked Mable if we could take a polaroid selfie with her. She was happy to do so, but she informed us that the birds could take the picture for us. We got together and a golden finch and cardinal took the picture for us. I can honestly say that I will never see that happen again. I was happy that we were able to get a picture with Mable. She did teach me a lot about the lessons you learn from quilting. We thanked her and headed next door to what she called "The Gift Shop."

13

The Gift Shop

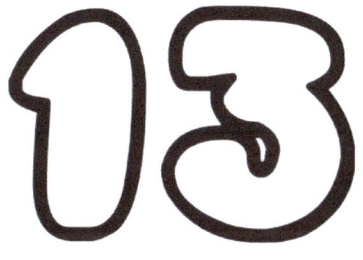

We took the cobblestone path full of birds to the street. We walked to the blue house next door, like Mable told us to. There was a flashing light in the window that said OMNIFICLAND Gift Shop. As we entered the house, a bell rang. It was the kind of bell you hear when you enter a store. Walking into the store we heard soft elevator type music. It truly looked like a gift shop. It had all kinds of post cards, t shirts and other touristy type items for OMNIFICLAND.   I know it is kind of cheesy, but I was hoping to get an OMNIFICLAND t shirt or something. I mean this has been a trip that I will never forget. I had to have some kind of souvenir.

Henley was thinking the same thing. He was looking through the post cards and smiling while he looked at each card. There were post cards of all the places we had visited in this place. Post cards for Black & White Circle, Lilac Lane, Boombox Cave, Writing Whereabouts, The Weeping Willows, Painted Dogs, Paintbrush Forest, Blue Dasher Dragon flies, Wool Transit, Quilter's Corner, and other places that we didn't go to. I was excited while I looked around the shop. There were stuffed plush toys of Sharpay, Pharrah the Phrase Fairy, The Eraser, Winslow Coolidge, Rizzo and other dogs.

There were things you could buy to create. There were magnets, keychains and all the things you see in gift shops. There was an OMNIFICLAND board game and playing cards. There were mini versions of the white chair that started this whole journey. I wish I could get some of these things. Henley and I kept showing each other fun finds in this cool place.

Suddenly we heard someone say, "Well I have customers!! How exciting! I am Neil. I get to run the gift shop here in OMNIFICLAND. How can I help you folks today?"

He had just stepped through one of those beaded doors. The beads were still swaying back and forth after he went through them.

"Hello, and nice to meet you Neil. My dad's favorite singer is Neil Diamond. You are the first Neil I have ever met." I said

He put his hands over his heart. "Oh, I just love Neil Diamond!" He began to sing "Far! You've been traveling far! Without a home, but not without a star. Create! Only want to create! On the roads and on a bus... Your coming to OMNIFICLAND!" he smiled at his change of words.

"Hi Neil. We were hoping you had some information for us about how to get home." Said Henley.

"The famous Iris and Henley, Right? Yes, you are famous here in OMNIFICLAND! I do have a secret passage for you to take out of here, but first you need to see something." Neil snapped his fingers and walked through the hanging beads into the back room.

We weren't quite sure what that meant. Were we supposed to follow him. We stood there and waited. He came right back and handed us both a flashlight. My flashlight was pink with sparkles on it. Henley's flashlight was green with blue stripes. They both said OMNIFICLAND on the side of them.

"You are going to need these. No charge! You need to follow the tunnel, which can get dark at times. The flashlights will help." Neil said.

We held the flashlights and waited for more directions. Neil walked to the back room again and came back with two prints of paintings. They were small prints, probably 5 by 7. Then were wrapped in plastic and had a matted frame. As soon as he handed them to us, I looked at mine with surprise.

I got emotional and teary eyed. It was the painting I had made in the Paintbrush Forest.

"How did you get these? I am so glad I have a copy!" I said happily.

Henley had his now too. I was thinking I would never get to see mine. I was very thankful to have it. It was something I was very proud of. Henley was pretty excited too.

"OMNIFICLAND knows true talent when it sees it. Your prints will be flying off the shelfs here soon. They are very good!" Neil complimented us.

We put our prints in our bags to keep them safe. I had to admit my bag was getting a little full. I had my quilt, print, snacks, OMNIFICLAND journal, polaroid camera, water, mixed tape and now a flashlight.

"They will be our number one seller right now. They are flying off the shelves. These are the best paintings we have had in here for quite some time now. I am glad to give you a complimentary print. You deserve it." Neil said with a smile.

Neil directed us to follow him. There was a shed in the back of the gift shop. He opened to door to tell us where to start. We thanked him and he headed back into the gift shop. After Neil left we looked down the long, dark tunnel. We turned out flashlights on and started down the tunnel. As we walked in the tunnel we talked about all the crazy things we had seen and all the fun things we got to do. We decided not to tell anyone about OMNIFICLAND. We thought it was something that you have to discover on your own.

"It is hard to believe we are getting close to home, to school." I stated.

"I know, I feel like it might be kind of weird going back. After seeing all the things we saw, it might feel weird to be back." Henley said.

I agreed with him. I mean when you think about it, we had done a lot of things no one would ever dream of. I also wondered if the adults at school had been to OMNIFICLAND. They had to have, right? I mean they sent us to OMNIFICLAND. I wonder how long it has existed. How many kids have visited there before.

"It is going to be hard to keep this secret. I know it is what we should do, but after visiting there it will be hard not to tell anyone." Henley said.

I also wondered where we would come back in the school. Will we end up back at the elevator? I am guessing that is what will take us back. It is crazy to think that we had been traveling for miles through all different kinds of lands, and now we are heading back to school. As we were walking through the tunnel, we both started to hear a voice. I asked Henley if he heard the voice. He did hear the voice and was wondering if I heard it too. I think it is coming from our back packs.

14 The Journal's Post Its

We stopped in the tunnel and looked in our back packs. We both looked at each other in amazement when we saw that our OMNIFICLAND journals were glowing. Mine was glowing pink and Henley's was glowing blue.

"Should we open them and see why they are glowing?" Henley asked.

I feel like they must be glowing for a reason. Maybe it had a message for us. I slowly opened my journal. I paged through the memories we had made here in OMNIFICLAND. Once I got past the last memory, there was a blank page. All of a sudden, a post it magically appeared on the page I was on. The same thing happened to Henley's journal. We looked at each other and then back at our journals. Suddenly words started to appear on the post its. It was like a to do list was being written.

To do – Saturday
- Work from 6 to 9
- Pay Bills
- House chores
- Mow the lawn
- Walk the dog
- Family Fun
- Build and paint bench for Tom.

To do – Saturday
- Get bills ready
- Laundry
- Clean House
- Dishes
- Groceries
- Spend time with family
- Work on quilt for Sue

Henley's post it had a list of things to do on Saturday and so did mine. I am pretty sure my post it was a list my mom and dad would make. Henley was thinking the same for his post it. I wondered why these magical post-its appeared. Was it trying to tell us something important before we headed home?

"My mom and dad always seem like they have so much to get done at home, especially on the weekends. I kind of give them a hard time about it. I hate to say it, but sometimes I make them feel bad about doing all the things they need to do. I can be pretty whiny." Henley said as if he was embarrassed.

"I kind of do the same thing to my parents. I know they get stressed out about money and just getting things done. They work so hard during the week that they have to do things on the weekend. I know they try hard to do family things, but I know I could complain less. I am sure it doesn't help their stresses." I said shamefully.

I got what the journals were trying to tell us. Family is important. I need to help out more. I know I can do that. I could help make that to do list smaller. Henley agreed. He wanted to help more at home too. I don't think kids realize how much stress parents have. Parents need to work, provide food and other things for the whole family to live. I never thought about this before but, we always have toilet paper. I never once have had to tell my parents to buy toilet paper. It is something they just do. I guess I can sometimes take things for granted. I know that is maybe a silly example, but it is true. There are so many things I do not have to think about because my parents do it for me. I always have toothpaste. I always have food. When I get sick, they get me medicine. My parents really are every day heroes. I know they have creative minds too, but they don't always get to create because of all the other things they need to do. Henley and I both looked at our lists and realized that they want to create too. The very last think on both lists had to do with a creation.

    I decided that I want to do better so that my parents can get to that last thing on the list. Being creative and using the imagination is good for the soul. I realize that sometimes I was preventing my parents from getting to create those things they really enjoy to make. I could be pretty selfish at times.

    I was glad that these messages came to us before leaving OMNIFICLAND. I understood the lesson being sent to us in this strange, but effective way. As Henley and I were discussing how we were going to do better, another post it wondrously appeared in our journals.

    This time we realized that we both had the same post its. This time there were three post its.

To do – Saturday HOME
- Pay Bills
- Clean house
- Laundry
- Walk the dog
- Grocery shopping
- Game for son
- Start school list if there is time

To do – Saturday if time
- Go to museum with family
- Refinish dresser
- Sew quilt
- Create fun stickers for school

To do – Saturday School
- Corrections
- Make copies for lesson
- Science lesson
- Create morning boards for the week
- Reading logs & journals

    Henley and I both got all three post its. We realized at the same time who they belonged to. Mrs. Pepper was a pretty busy lady. She is always doing her best to have things organized and ready for us. She is always happy, even though she has a million things to get done. We could see that she really likes to create too. Unfortunately, because of her long school and home list, she probably doesn't get to create much.

    Mrs. Pepper was the teacher that sent us both to OMNIFICLAND. She could see talent in us. She knew the perfect time to send us. I mean I had doodled on my paper several times, but she didn't send me to OMNIFICLAND until today.

    She knew when I needed these important lessons. Same with Henley. She knew exactly when he needed to learn these essential lessons. I was so happy that I was able to go on the journey with Henley. I think it would've been completely changed without him. I knew that we would be close friends for a long time because we shared this amazing, art expedition together.

    I realized that I needed to listen to Mrs. Pepper more intently. She always said to make sure we were showing "active listening". Now I really understood what that meant. Listen activity and with meaningful intent. Listen as though you really care about what the person is saying. Teachers really should get an award every year for trying to get kids to learn the lessons they need to learn. Not all kids are nice and not all kids deserve a nice teacher like Mrs. Pepper. She never complains though, even when some kids are mean and totally disrespectful to her. She never loses her cool. I always wonder if she ever gets mad. I don't think I have ever seen her show anger. She is disappointed at times, but never mean. We put our journals away and continued on the tunnel path. We were still using our flashlights because it was still pretty dark.

The tunnel seemed to go on forever. Just as we were talking about how far we were walking, the tunnel started to get lighter. We were coming to an end of the tunnel. We came to a dead end. There was a small ladder on the wall where the dead end came. We must need to climb it. Henley went first to check it out. He took six steps up the ladder and went through an opening in the ceiling.

"Oh my gosh! We did it! We made it back to the elevator. Come on, climb up." Henley said.

I climbed up the six steps and peaked through the ceiling. Henley was standing in this room waiting for me. I looked around and recognized the room. It was very similar to the elevator room that was in Mrs. Grizzly's office. There was an elevator in the small room. On the wall next to the elevator was the word SCHOOL. I was guessing that this elevator would take us back to school. At least that is what we were hoping. There was only one button for this elevator. It was a circle button with the word GRIZZLY on it. That was it!

We were going back to school. I couldn't believe we were finally back to a somewhat normal and familiar place. Henley pushed the button and the doors opened. We stepped inside. The elevator traveled up for about 2 minutes. It was crazy to think that in just a few minutes we would be back at school. I wondered how long we had been gone. Did anyone notice that we were gone for so long.

15

Mrs. Pepper's Lesson

The elevator stopped. Henley and I were excited. We waited patiently for the door to open. When it opened, we were right where we thought we would end up. We were right where this all started. The elevator in Mrs. Grizzly's office was right on the other side of the small door. Just as we stepped out of the elevator, Mrs. Grizzly stepped into the small room.

"Hello kids. How was your adventure? I hope you learned something that will stay with you for a long time." Said Mrs. Grizzly.

"Hi Mrs. Grizzly. We had an AMAZING adventure. Thanks for sending us on it." Said Henley.

"Yes, thank you!" I said. "How long have we been gone? It felt like we were gone for days." I asked.

"OMNIFICLAND time is different than our time. You only have been gone for two hours. I know it seems crazy but you have seen a lot of crazy things today. Before you can head back to class, you need to visit with someone. Come with me." Demanded Mrs. Grizzly.

We followed her and stepped through the small, corner door and into her office. Mrs. Pepper was in the office waiting for us. She smiled at us as Mrs. Grizzly exited the office. She shut the door behind her as she left. We sat down at the table with Mrs. Pepper.

"Thank you, Mrs. Pepper, for sending us to OMNIFICLAND. What made you send us to OMNIFICLAND?" asked Henley.

"Well Henley, you are very talented. So are you Iris. I could see that you needed to explore the arts in a way to help grow your confidence of your craft." Said Mrs. Pepper.

I wasn't sure what to say. I just know that I was SO thankful that she sent me to OMNIFICLAND. I had learned so much from all of the characters I met. I also learned that Mrs. Pepper does things for a reason. Her actions are helpful and kind. I went to her and gave her a big hug.

"Mrs. Pepper, I want to thank you for helping me really see some things clearly. I know how hard you work. You really are one of the best teachers ever!" I expressed my thoughts to her.

"We need to have a talk. You cannot tell anyone about your journey today. I know that you probably want to share a lot of different things with your parents, friends and family. OMNIFICLAND has been around for a long time. It has helped many people. One of the main reasons it has lived on is because people have kept this special secret. It is important to learn from all the characters you met. It is essential to teach others through your actions. As long as you can keep this secret, you can take your backpack, shoes, and other souvenirs with you. Do you think you can do that?" Mrs. Pepper asked us.

Henley and I looked at each other and nodded yes. We understood what Mrs. Pepper was saying and we knew it was important to do what she said. It would be hard to keep this secret. I would do it for Mrs. Pepper

though. She is always trying to teach us life lessons. She has these 5 rules posted in her classroom.
1. Help others see their talents.
2. Don't criticize people.
3. Grow in your craft or passion every day.
4. Treat others with kindness.
5. Be Patient.

"Remember that OMNIFICLAND is a place but it is also a feeling. A feeling of knowing your talent and sharing it in the best way you can. I have something for each of you. I got one of these when I traveled to OMNIFICLAND years ago. It is something that will remind you of this magical place. It will be something that will stay with you forever." Explained Mrs. Pepper.

"Did you kids know that when I was your age, I was sent to OMNIFICLAND. It was such an amazing journey. It is something that I have remembered for years! I want you to have these." Said Mrs. Pepper as she handed us two buttons.

The buttons said, I have been to OMNIFICLAND. They were unique buttons. They were colorful and personal to each of us. My button had my tree house painting on it along with a quilt. Henley's button had a boom box with music notes.

"When I see talent in my classroom, I send you on your way. Mrs. Grizzly and Mrs. Walker have also been to OMNIFICLAND. Many kids and adults have visited, but no one talks of it. Help me keep these lessons coming for many people. You can do that by just staying quiet. I know you will." Said Mrs. Pepper.

Right after she said this, she opened her blazer jacket. On the inside was a button that said I Have been to OMNIFICLAND. She winked at us.

Her button was yellow. It had a stack of books and a pencil on it. I knew that when we went back to class that I would have friends asking me where I had been. Mrs. Pepper said that I could tell them that I was helping Mrs. Walker with something. I didn't feel right about not being honest, but I also knew how important it was to keep OMNIFICLAND a secret.

"You have been added to the True Hallway of Artists now. Your name is on the work. You may get some questions. Just be honest about how you painted the art. That is all you have to do. It is time to head back. I bet you will pay a little closer attention now when you head down the long hallway in our school." Smiled Mrs. Pepper.

Henley and I grabbed our bags and headed out of Mrs. Grizzly's office. As we stepped out into the hallway, I saw the white chair. I had to stop and look at it. It is where it all started. I had an appreciation for the white chair now. Henley stopped to look too. I knew he knew what was on my mind. He felt the same way.

We continued past Mrs. Walker's secretary desk. She smiled at us, bigger than she ever had before. She knew what was going on and she was happy for us. She gave us each a big hug and then told us to head back to class. We continued to class. We walked down the long hallway or "The Hallway of Artists" according to Mrs. Pepper.

    I paid close attention to each painting that we passed. I didn't realize how many paintings were hanging, until now. Just as we got to about the center of the hall I noticed my painting.

True Hallway of Artists

    My painting was in the Hallway of Artists? This painting was supposed to depict my past, present and future. When we were in the Paintbrush Forest I had to think of something quickly that would express my feelings through paint. It needed to express my passions and the things I loved. I painted a three-tiered tree house. I decided to paint the tree house because we have one in our yard. My dad built us one and my sisters and I love to play in it. There is a tree going through the center of it. Playing in it always makes me feel at home and free to create. That tree house makes my sisters and I happy, so that is why I decided to paint a tree house. Each tier that I painted in the tree house stood for my past, present and future. On each tier I painted things that I was passionate about.

    The bottom tier was all about my family and the things they learned from my grandparents. I painted their talents and passions. On the second tier I painted the things that I enjoy creating right now. I also made sure to depict the importance of my family. The top tier was all about the things I look forward to creating and being. I had the most fun painting the tree, because it was beautiful. It was strong. It held all three tiers of the tree house together. My name, Iris Jonas was in the top right corner of my painting. Looking at my art in this long hallway made me happy. I felt like I knew myself better. I was proud of myself.

I hadn't seen Henley's painting yet. He was a few feet away looking at his own painting. I walked over to him to see it. It was so colorful. It was totally Henley. I saw footprints and it looked as though they were dancing. His use of color was amazing. The bright colors really popped because he used a black and navy background. Henley Roberts was painted in the corner with bright yellow.

"Nice job Henley! I love the color. I think this painting is you! I can see you in it." I told him.

"Thanks Iris. Isn't it crazy to see our art in the hallway? You know I have walked by the paintings in this hall so many times. Now we know that they are actually paintings people painted in OMNIFICLAND." Pointed out Henley.

We walked slowly down the hall and looked at all the paintings. They were all unique and different in their own way. I noticed something as we got near the end of the hall. There was a simple painting of a book on a table. There was also an apple sitting on the table next to the book. The word TEACH was painted on the book. There was a tiny signature in the bottom corner that said Joyce Pepper. I knew just by looking at this modest and remarkable painting, who had painted it.

Henley could tell as well. He smiled and simply said, "Mrs. Pepper."

I smiled too. I could just imagine Mrs. Pepper in OMNIFICLAND. No wonder she seemed so wise. She really is a great teacher. I knew that every time I walked down this hallway, I would pay attention better. These were true pieces of art that needed courtesy and care.

One of the paintings that popped out to me was one of the dog Rizzo from the Painted Dogs House. It was so obvious that it was him. There was a familiar name in the corner of the painting. It said Winslow. Could it be that Winslow Coolidge went to school here? How cool is that?

We knew we couldn't gawk at the painting the rest of the day. Henley and I continued back to the classroom. We were surprised to see that no one really said anything when we returned to the room. Everyone seemed to be working on a reading assignment. The assignment they were working on was sitting on our desks. Mrs. Pepper was walking the room and helping students that needed assistance. She is probably the most organized teacher I have ever known. You always knew what to do when you walked into the room. Mrs. Pepper always had directions and clear expectations on the board. Everyone was always busy. One thing that I always appreciated about Mrs. Pepper's class is that everyone was in different places of learning and that was okay.

The timer at the front of the room told us that there was only 5 minutes left until recess. I was excited to go outside and just play. I got to work on my reading for the five minutes remaining. Typically, I would kind of waste time a little and doodle on my paper. I decided to get my work done first. I wanted to make Mrs. Pepper proud. I know she didn't care if I doodled, but I think I learned that there is a time for everything. The first thing I need to do is what is expected. I saw Henley working hard too. Mrs. Pepper always let us doodle or draw if we got done with our work. I was going to do it the right way and in the right order without giving Mrs. Pepper any trouble.

Coming back into the classroom kind of reminded me of the movie Back to the Future. When Marty McFly came back to the present after going to the past, he saw things in a different was because of what he had experienced when he time traveled. I was truly seeing things in an altered way. It wasn't a bad way. It was just a way for me to appreciate the people in my world and the roles they played in my life. Just as I was thinking about all of this, the timer went off.

doodle here

The Kindness of a Rock

All the kids started to clear their desks to get ready for recess. We stood up at our desks to show Mrs. Pepper that we were ready for our recess break. Mrs. Pepper then dismissed us to recess. We all walked out to the playground. Henley and I gravitated towards each other once we got outside. We decided to just walk around and we watched what was happening around us. As we were walking, I noticed a girl in our class that looked sad. She was sitting on a bench by herself. Her name is Sophia. I had never noticed her alone before, but today she seemed pretty down. I had an idea. I told Henley what I was thinking. He agreed that it was a great idea. I quickly found the teacher on recess duty. I asked her if I could go inside quick. Usually teachers don't let us go back inside, but I had to try.

Surprisingly, the teacher let me go back in. I went to my OMNIFICLAND bag. I had put it in my back pack before going back into the class earlier. I grabbed one of the rocks I had gotten from the Painted Rock River. It was a yellow smiley rock. I figured maybe it would make her smile. Henley waited outside for me as I got the rock. As I looked at the rock, I smiled. Just looking at it, I felt like I was back in OMNIFICLAND. It took me back to when I picked it up. I snapped out of my imagination and left the coatroom. I put the rock in my pocket. I walked back to Henley, who looked excited to give the rock to Sophia. As I approached Henley, his face was saying are you ready? I nodded to him. Together we walked to the bench where Sophia was sitting. She was kicking her feet and looking at the ground. We sat on each side of her and looked at her. She looked back and forth between the two of us. She wasn't quite sure what to think.

"Hey Sophia! How are you?" I asked.

Sophia got upset. I think she thought we were teasing her or making fun of her. She stopped kicking her feet and looked at her lap.

"Henley and I wanted to come over and see if you were okay." I said.

"Yeah! We thought you looked down. Do you need some cheer?" asked Henley.

She started to look as though she might cry.

"Maggie and Kayley are being mean. I feel it is easier to just ignore them, but then I get sad. Why do they have to be mean? I didn't do anything to them." Sophia complained.

I could tell this really made her upset. This was something that must happen often. She seemed fed up and tired of the actions of her friends.

"Iris has something that could cheer you up." Henley said with a little excitement.

"When I was on a trip recently, I found something that made me smile. I took it with me, thinking that maybe I would need it to help me smile again someday. I think that maybe you should have it." I said to Sophia.

I put my hand in my pocket and pulled out the painted rock. I thought about how the ERASER was mean, but really just wanted someone to care. I am sure Sophia's friends just need a little love too.

Sophia took the bright yellow rock from my hand. She brushed the smiley face with her fingers. As she looked at the rock, a smile appeared on her face.

"How did you know?" asked Sophia.

"Know what?" Asked Henley.

Sophia explained that about a month ago her grandfather died. She was really close to him. He was an amazing painter. When she would visit him, he would teach her how to paint. About a week before he died, she went to see him. His health was going downhill quickly and she was worried that she would lose him. Her grandfather could see her worry and invited her to come paint with her. The last think they painted together were rocks. She said it was a memory that would stick with her forever.

"Getting this rock from you today, it means a lot. I feel it is my grandfather's message to keep my head up. To keep smiling. Thank you, Iris, and thank you Henley." Sophia said with a smile and a tear in her eye.

"Sophia, can I ask you something?" asked Henley.

"Sure." She said.

"What was your grandfather's name?" Henley asked with curiosity.

"He was the BEST grandpa any girl could ask for. His name was Randy, Randy Rawls." Said Sophia.

Henley and I looked at each other and smiled.

I felt good knowing that I had made Sophia feel better. What a coincidence. We just gave her a rock from her grandfather's Painted Rock River in OMNIFCLAND. I sensed that I should go further with this. I thought of the ERASER.

"Not everyone is bad, and even the bad want to feel loved. Maybe you can teach a lesson to those who need love too." I suggested to Sophia.

She understood what I was saying. She nodded and put the rock in her pocket. She asked if we wanted to play, and of course we said yes. We played the rest of the recess. We all laughed and ran around as we pretended to be on an adventure.

Sophia stopped in the middle of playing and said, "Can I ask you guys a question?"

We both nodded our heads yes.

"Why are you both wearing white shoes with black drawing on them? Is it the new, in thing? Sophia wondered.

Henley and I had forgotten that we were still wearing the white loafers. We looked at each other, then our shoes and then back at each other and laughed. "I guess we just like the same kind of shoes, but they are pretty fun, right?" Henley said.

The best part of recess was when the bell rang. We all lined up at the door. Sophia walked over to the girls that were being mean to her. She took the rock out of her pocket and gave it to them. They both smiled at her. The rock kind of fixed everything she was dealing with. After giving them the rock, she ran back to Henley and I. Sophia was excited as she ran over to us.

I just talked with them and said I wanted to start a rock painting club. They said they wanted to. You guys started this whole thing, you should help me get it going. You really helped me today. I want to help others, like you helped me. We should come up with a name and get it all ready to present to Mrs. Pepper or the principal. I bet Mrs. Pepper would help us.

"What if we create a "Painted Rock River? Anyone can get a rock when they need one." Suggested Henley.

"I love that idea. How did you think of that Henley?" asked Sophia.

Henley and I looked at each other and smiled. I knew exactly where his idea had come from.

"There is a perfect place on the playground to put this river. What about over by the swings? We could wind it around to that tree. It will be perfect." I said.

"Thanks again for making my day guys. I am excited to see what happens next." Sophia followed the line in after our visit.

OMNIFICLAND had already made such a difference on how I looked at things. This Painted Rock Club would be fun. It would help kids create, and most importantly it would teach kids to be kind. We were all really excited to see what Mrs. Pepper would say about it.

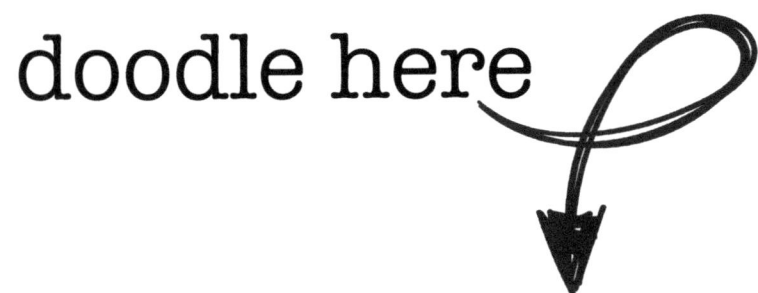

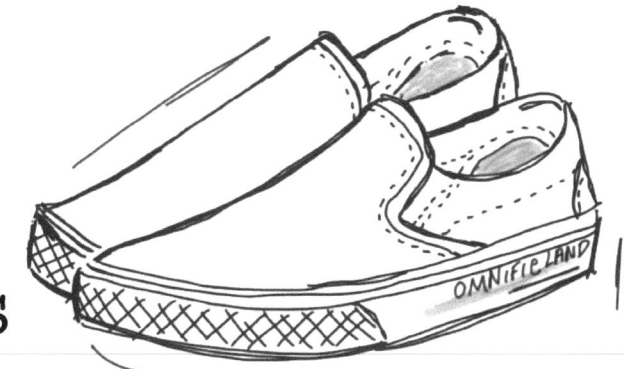

Lesson from the Loafers

On my way home from school I thought about my day. I was wearing my white loafers, and I was carrying my backpack on my shoulders. Inside my backpack was the OMNIFICLAND bag I had gotten. Inside it were treasures I had no clue about at the beginning of my day. I wondered if my sisters would wonder where my loafers came from. I decided that when I got home, I would put them in a safe place. My sisters and I walked home, like usual. When we got home, I went to my room and put my OMNIFICLAND things in my hope chest. I didn't want anything happening to my treasures. I laid on my bed after I got my things in a secret place. It was nice to just relax and think about my day.

"Iris! Iris!" my mom yelled.

I woke up to my mom yelling my name. I must have been pretty tired from such a long day, or was it all a dream? I looked at my feet and saw I was still wearing my loafers. It was real. I really went to OMNIFICLAND.

"Iris, supper!" I heard my mom say again.

"Coming mom!" I yelled back.

I was actually really hungry. I wondered what was for supper. I walked upstairs to the kitchen. Everyone was around the table waiting for me. Mom had made her famous spaghetti. This was turning out to be the best day ever. I sat down and filled my plate with noodles and yummy sauce. We all talked about our day. We all ate. It was nice to be home and I was so happy to have my favorite meal. I thanked my mom for making the meal. After we finished, it was time to do dishes. My sisters and I are in charge of this chore. It is not too bad. I get to spend time with my sisters and for the most part we have fun doing them. It felt good to do something normal.

After about half the dishes were done, I ran to the bathroom quick. Of course, my sisters thought I was trying to get out of doing them, but I really did have to go. As I got to the bathroom, my mom called me into her bedroom. She asked me how my day was.

"Did anything exciting happen at school today?" she asked me as if she knew something.

"It was good." I responded nervously.

"Did you get a new pair of shoes?" She asked me.

I got nervous. What would I tell her? Would she believe me if I told her about OMNIFICLAND? I wasn't sure what to say.

"Um, I um won them at school." I said

My mom seemed to be curious about the shoes. She asked me to come in and shut the bedroom door.

"I have another question for you. How was Mable? Did you get to use the squigger?" she asked.

What? Could this be? Had my mom been to OMNIFICLAND? I looked at my mom with wonder.

"What are you talking about mom?" I asked innocently.

"Can I show you something? You must keep it quiet. Can you do that?" she asked me very seriously.

I feel like a lot of people were asking me to keep quiet today.

"I can keep quiet." I said.

My mom went into her closet. She dug way in the back and took out a shoe box. What in the world was going to be in this box? She opened the box. She slowly and carefully took out a pair of white loafers. The loafers had 6 flowers and 4 tallies. Just like mine. She also pulled out her artist mixed tape from the box. She had an OMNIFICLAND journal and a button that said I have been to OMNIFICLAND.

"Mom! I went there today. It was amazing. The people, the creations, the creatures, the art!! I just loved it. I am so glad I can talk to you about this." I said excitedly.

"Sshhh! Your sisters will hear. You must have had an amazing day. I hope that you learned from the people and things you saw today. Iris, you are so unbelievably talented. I love you!" mom said with such love.

"I love you too Mom!" I said.

"We are given beauty every day. We just need to pay attention and notice how truly blessed we are with it." Said mom.

This was so true, and this was something that I realized today on my journey. I now have opened my eyes and seen the true splendor in all things.

doodle here

Mural of Mistakes

    My sisters and I share a room. We always listen to music as we fall asleep. It is something that calms us all. We also have multi colored Christmas lights in our room. My sisters and I sometimes talk while we are winding down. That night I lay in bed and I thought about all the lessons I learned in the day. One of the most important things I learned was to create without question. It is okay to make mistakes. We learn from our mistakes. That is something that Mrs. Pepper always told us too. I thought about how I was nervous about OMNIFICLAND, but in the end it was all good. I know I need to learn to trust more. I tend to worry a lot. I don't know why I do that, but I do.

    As I thought of all of these things, I fell asleep hard. When I sleep is when I come up with a lot of good ideas. I even keep a notepad by my bed for any good night time thoughts. As I slept I thought about mistakes. I thought about painting and I thought about making mistakes a positive thing. Suddenly I woke up with a great idea. I jotted down my thoughts. I was really excited about what I came up with. I was going to share it with Mrs. Pepper as soon as I got to school tomorrow. I couldn't believe I fell back asleep, but I did. After a good night sleep, I woke up and got ready very quickly. I ate a bowl of Kix and then ran to get my notebook next to my bed. I grabbed my idea and asked my sisters to hurry up.

"Why are you in such a hurry?" asked my sister Mandy.

"I am just excited for school." I answered.

We all walked out the door and trudged to school. I thought about my idea that I was going to get to share. I was excited to tell Henley too. I walked to the coatroom and hung up my backpack. I grabbed my idea notebook and headed to the classroom. My classmates were trickling in and starting the morning tasks. I checked the board to see what was expected. Mrs. Pepper always had a morning board up to keep us on task. It also gave her a chance to tell everyone good morning.

I really wanted to talk to Mrs. Pepper, but I knew that it wasn't the right time. I figured I would talk to her at morning recess. I worked hard all morning in math and reading. It was crazy how much I wanted to please Mrs. Pepper. After knowing that she too had been to OMNIFICLAND and that she sent me because she saw talent in me. I wanted to do my best. It seemed like forever, but recess was finally here. Mrs. Pepper told us to stand and clear desks to show we were ready for recess. I had a bit of a knot in my stomach because I was eager to talk to Mrs. Pepper about my idea. We walked out to the playground. Mrs. Pepper walked out with us. All the kids ran to play, but I stayed back to share my idea.

"Mrs. Pepper, can I talk to you about something?" I asked her nervously.

"Of course you can Iris. What's up?" She asked.

"I have an idea that I would like to make come to life for our school. I thought of it last night after visiting OMNIFICLAND." I said.

Mrs. Pepper seemed interested. I think she could tell that I was nervous. I shared my thoughts and she was really excited about what I had to share. She told me she would talk with the principal and other teachers, but she felt they would love it.

I felt wonderful and I was so glad that I was able to build up enough confidence to ask her about it.

After recess, we finished reading and then went to lunch. I didn't tell anyone else about what I shared with Mrs. Pepper. I didn't even tell Henley yet. I didn't want to share until I knew for sure it would happen. Surprisingly, as I was eating lunch Mrs. Pepper asked me to go with her to the office. Mrs. Grizzly and Mrs. Pepper wanted to talk to me about my idea. Mrs. Grizzly said she was so happy I came up with it. They decided that they would make it happen. They had talked about a perfect place for us to display it. There was a big blank wall near the lunch room that a lot of the kids and visitors would see it.

Mrs. Grizzly said, "I would like you to share all your thinking on this Iris. How do you see this working?"

I was so happy to share my thoughts. "I would like to have a large area where we focus on our mistakes we make. I feel we often focus on only what turns out good or perfect. We need to realize that mistakes are great! They are almost better than being perfect. We learn from our mistakes. We should put them on display. I thought we could call it,

MURAL OF MISTAKES. I think it would be neat to paint the wall all different colors and in random patterns. Then we should paint MURAL OF MISTAKES at the top. Then we post our mistakes on the mural." I said with conviction.

I had practiced this explanation in my head several times since I thought of it last night. Both Mrs. Grizzly and Mrs. Pepper were giddy with excitement.

"You have really learned a lot from going to OMNIFICLAND! Did you know that many of things you see around the school were created by students after they went to OMNIFICLAND. It truly just brings the best out of everyone. Everyone learns different lessons according to their own talents. Our True Hallway of Artists was created by a student." Said Mrs. Grizzly.

"And did you know that we had a student come to us with an idea inspired by you?" said Mrs. Pepper.

"Really? Who? What is the idea?" I said excitedly.

"Sophia Rawls came to me yesterday and asked if we could start a Rock Painting Club. She said that you and Henley helped her feel better with the gift of a simple painted rock. It is really great that you noticed that she needed some cheering up." Said Mrs. Pepper.

"We think this is a great club for students to create, learn and share kindness. We even want to create a Kindness Rock River on the playground. We will have a time that kids can create painted rocks every week. Those rocks can go in the river. Students can be cheered up daily with these message painted rocks." Mrs. Grizzly said with enthusiasm.

    I was filled with hope that these two artsy things were going to happen at our school all because of what Henley and I experienced yesterday.

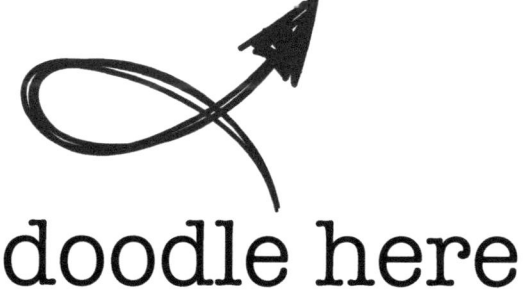

20

Perfecting Our Craft

    I raced to find Henley at lunch recess. I was going a mile a minute as I told him about the two ideas that were going to come to life all because of us. Henley was excited and seemed to even get a bit emotional as I was telling him.
    "I can't believe it! Do you remember when we told our wishes to the Blue Dasher Dragon Flies?" I asked.
    "Yes, I do." I said.
    "My wish came true! I wished that our real world (at school) could become more creative like OMNIFICLAND. I wished that we could create more at school. So, my wish came true!" He said.
    "I guess my wish came true too, because I wished that people would be more kind to each other. I think Sophia learned that yesterday as she asked her bullies to start a Rock Painting Club." I realized and said with excitement.
    I thought about how many creative experiences had happened for me yesterday. Creating is really a way to release stress and enjoy the beauty of everyday things. Everyone is creative in different ways. I wondered what else I could do to share this thought with others. I thought of a quote

that could be added to the Mural of Mistakes wall. I knew it would work perfectly and help people see the true beauty of mistakes.

"We make mistakes as we create. Those mistakes are the true beauty that help us grow artistically. Own your mistakes with passion. Be proud of them. Only those mistakes help us see our true talents."
                                                                            Iris Jonas

    I wouldn't have been able to come up with this quote without visiting OMNIFICLAND. The people and places in OMNIFICLAND helped me to grow in art. I realize that everyone has their own skills that they accumulate as they live and learn. I am lucky enough to have a family that has given me familiarity of many ways to create. When you grow up with talented people to guide you, you mature in talent just being with them.
    I know not all people are as lucky as I am to be surrounded by these idols of talent. I feel it is my job to help those people grow and see their own beauty. I am so very thankful that Mrs. Pepper handed me that OMNIFICLAND card. She saw my talent and became one of the people that would nurture and encourage my creative hand.
    I am not sure if it is possible to visit OMNIFICLAND again, but I would love to go back someday. It is really a true gift of a place. It taught me to appreciate the people in my life and treat them the best that I can. I hope that it lives on forever to help cheer young artists on a journey to genuine compassion for art.

Lessons the author hopes you took from this book.

1. Try your best, even when things are hard.
2. Believe in yourself always.
3. Your teachers see your talents and strengths.
4. Learn from every moment of your day.
5. Think about your choices before you make them.
6. Follow your heart.
7. Be kind to others.
8. Learn from your personal idols.
9. Ask questions.
10. Grow in your craft or passion every day.
11. Help out when you can.
12. Capture special moments in your life.
13. See beauty in simple things.
14. Stand up for yourself.
15. Use your imagination.
16. Help others see their talents.
17. Don't criticize people. You don't know their story.
18. Be patient.
19. Take pride in your own art.
20. Learn from your mistakes. They make us who we are.

Printed in the USA
CPSIA information can be obtained
at www.ICGtesting.com
LVHW070721100923

757647LV00064B/352

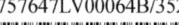